SUMMER

MEDITATIONS

SUMMER
MEDITATIONS

Václav Havel

**Translated from the Czech
by Paul Wilson**

Vintage Books
A Division of Random House, Inc.
New York

FIRST VINTAGE BOOKS EDITION, JUNE 1993

Library of Congress Cataloging-in-Publication Data

Havel, Václav.
[Letní přemítání. English]
Summer meditations / Václav Havel; translated
from the Czech by Paul Wilson.
p.   cm.
Originally published: New York: A.A. Knopf, 1992.
ISBN 0-679-74497-5 (pbk.)
1. Czechoslovakia — Politics and government — 1989–
2. Political ethics. I. Title.
[DB2241.H28A5   1993]
943.704'3 — dc20   92-50602
CIP

Manufactured in the United States of America

10 9 8 7 6 5 4 3 2 1

Contents

Preface
to the Vintage edition of
Summer Meditations

I WROTE this book in 1991 during a ten-day holiday. I felt the need to reflect on the political situation in our country, on our problems and our prospects. I also wanted to give an account of my opinions. Of course, a lot has changed since I wrote the book. When this new edition of *Summer Meditations* comes out in the United States, our country, Czechoslovakia, will no longer exist. We have divided and become two countries. Nevertheless, this is not just a book about how I had hoped the federation would hold together and how I fought for it, but also about what I wanted and how I thought at the time.

Václav Havel
Prague, November 20, 1992

Translator's Preface

S UMMER *Meditations* belongs to a rare genre: a political testament written by a highly respected politician while still in office. It is, moreover, *not* a collection of occasional speeches but a profound reflection on the nature and practice of politics by a man who, until November 1989, was a marginalized and banned author in his own country, and who wrote about himself and his society from a perspective that sometimes included the prison cell. This is Václav Havel's first book as president of the Czech and Slovak Federal Republic. I believe it to be a work of great importance, for it helps us to understand in intimate detail the problems and the promise in the post-Communist world.

The English-language edition of *Summer Meditations* differs from the Czech, *Letní přemítání*, in three ways. First, the present Chapter One, "Politics, Morality, and Civility", together with the present Epilogue, were the final chapter of the original text.

Second, because the political situation in Czechoslovakia, and indeed in the world, has changed since the book was written last summer, small amounts of new factual material have been added. Some of this material is based on consultations with President Havel's advisers, and some of it comes from a written interview I conducted with him in February 1992. Such changes occur chiefly in Chapter Two, on domestic politics, and Chapter Four, on foreign policy.

Third, wherever the original text contains references a Czech or Slovak reader would be expected to know, but for which an English-speaking reader might require an explanation, I have provided a background note at the end of the book, keyed to words or phrases in the main text. When such references could be explained in a word or two, I have done so directly in the text, in the form of an "invisible footnote". My background notes also indicate passages that differ substantially from the original text.

While the book's perspective in time is sometimes shifted by those interventions, none of the changes — as President Havel points out in his foreword — alters the book in any fundamental way. They are simply intended to make this extraordinary work, written by an extraordinary man in an extraordinary time, as accessible to English-speaking readers as it is to the Czechs and Slovaks for whom it was originally intended.

IN THE course of working on this translation, I have come to owe a great deal to many people whose help, advice, and co-operation were essential in bringing this work to completion. My thanks to Louise Dennys and Gena Gorrell for their meticulous editing and countless helpful ideas; to Bobbie Bristol and Frank Pike for their support; to Barbara Epstein for her enthusiasm and her useful editorial suggestions; to friends and colleagues who helped with information or advice — in particular, H. Gordon Skilling, Olga Stankovičová, Miroslav Scholz and Max Clarkson; and to Angelique Heerdink, who let me read her recent paper on the Slovak struggle for self-government.

In Czechoslovakia, my thanks go especially to Vladimír

Hanzel, President Havel's private secretary, for acting as go-between with the president and coming up with quick, accurate answers for my questions; to Anna Freimanová of Aura-Pont Agency, President Havel's literary agent in Prague, for help in contractual matters and in communicating with President Havel; and to Michael Žantovský, the president's spokesman, Miroslav Zámečník, director of the Centre for Economic Analysis in the office of the president, Tom Bridle from the president's Foreign Policy Department, and Jaroslav Šafařík, adviser to the president on matters pertaining to legislation and the civil service, all of whom were invaluable in providing information for the background notes and in checking the accuracy of my interpretation of certain passages in the text; and to the editor of the Czech edition of this book, Jan Zelenka of the Odeon Publishing House, who kindly read the English text and made many useful last-minute suggestions. I owe a special debt of gratitude to Václav Havel himself, who found time in his hectic schedule this February to answer my supplementary questions.

Finally, my thanks to my wife, Helena, and my son, Jake, for bearing with me during the last few months, when I must have seemed more absent than present.

Paul Wilson
Toronto, March 1992

Foreword

THESE meditations were inspired by conversations I had with Pavel Tigrid and Michael Žantovský, who prodded me into setting my thoughts down. To both of these men, I owe my thanks. I wrote the meditations at the end of July and the beginning of August 1991, and edited them at the end of August. Then, in late February of this year — in view of the momentous changes that had meanwhile taken place in the Soviet Union, and also in view of the resistance some of my proposals had met with in our Parliament — I reviewed some of the contents of this book especially for the English-language edition. Some of my comments have been integrated into the text.

I should say, however, that in fundamental things — in my concept of politics, in how I see its inner spirit — absolutely nothing has changed. I still see things and feel about things as I did when I wrote the final chapter of this book. Naturally, faced with the increasing complications of our public life at home, I have become aware of how immensely difficult it is to be guided in practice by the principles and ideals in which I believe. But I have not abandoned them in any way.

Václav Havel
Prague, March 1992

Introduction

WHEN the idea first came up that I should let my name stand for president of Czechoslovakia, it seemed like an absurd joke. All my life I had opposed the powers that be. I had never held political office, not even for a moment. I had always placed great store in my independence, and I had never liked anything too serious, too ceremonial, too official. Suddenly, I was on the way to holding an official position and, moreover, the highest in the land.

Slightly less than a month after this shocking proposal was put to me, I was unanimously elected president of my country. It happened quickly and unexpectedly, almost overnight one could say, giving me little time to prepare myself and my thoughts for the job. (I remember that a few short hours before the great demonstration at which Jiří Bartoška, on behalf of Civic Forum and the Public Against Violence, declared my candidacy, I had not yet made up my mind to accept. I will refrain from naming the friends whose arguments finally persuaded me.)

It might be said that I was swept into office by the revolution.

When I think about it today with a cool head, and after the passage of time, I find myself somewhat surprised that I was so surprised. After all, when I get involved in something (in my usual all-out manner) I often find myself at the head of it before long — not because I am more clever or more ambitious than the rest, but because I seem to get along with people, to be able to reconcile and unite them, to act as a sort of unifying agent. So it was only part of the natural course of events that although I had no formal position in Civic Forum I was perceived as the central figure, and when the Communist power structure crumbled so quickly, and even the president of the republic resigned at our request, I was asked to become a candidate for the office.

Although I believe I have foresight in other matters, I displayed a surprising lack of perspicacity where I myself was concerned.

Nevertheless, I did not hesitate for long, and not just because there was no time for hesitation, but also because I understood the task as an extension of what I had done before — that is, a natural continuation of my former civic involvement and my activities in the revolutionary events of 1989. It simply seemed to me that, since I had been saying A for so long, I could not refuse to say B; it would have been irresponsible of me to criticize the Communist regime all my life and then, when it finally collapsed (with some help from me), refuse to take part in the creation of something better.

My first term as president was brief, from December 29, 1989, to June 5, 1990. I understood that as a temporary period of service to our cause, and I didn't spend much time worrying about whether I was right for the job, or whether I enjoyed doing it; in the atmosphere of general enthusiasm over our new freedom, so quickly and elegantly won, I was simply "pulled forward by Being". With no embarrassment, no stage fright, no hesitation, I did everything I had to do. I was capable of speaking extempore (I who had never before spoken in public!) to several packed public squares a day, of negotiating confidently with the heads of great powers, of addressing foreign parliaments, and so on. In short, I was able to behave as masterfully as if I had been prepared and schooled for the presidency all my life. This was not because historical opportunity suddenly uncovered in me some special aptitude for the office, but because I became "an instrument of the time". That special time caught me up in its wild vortex and — in the absence of leisure to reflect on the matter — compelled me to do what had to be done. My wife had the same experience: I was pleasantly surprised at the matter-of-factness with which she, who had persistently opposed my standing for the office, accepted her new position and all the duties that went with it. She found her own public identity and work, and did not let it affect her in any adverse way. Others in my position would have done the same thing, though perhaps in different ways. There was no choice. History — if I may put it this way — forged ahead and through me, guiding my activities.

My second election was also preceded by few hesitations. I was the only candidate. I was nominated by the forces that had clearly won the elections, and the opposition did not oppose them in this matter. I made no personal effort to be elected, nor did I do anything to prevent it. Had I refused to run a second time I would have been generally perceived as abandoning the battlefield, if not actually forsaking a job undertaken. Thus my second term in office was again, in a sense, a mere extension of the first, its logical continuation, a fulfilment of the task I had already assumed: to help this country move from totalitarianism to democracy, from satellitehood to independence, from a centrally directed economy to market economics.

Today the situation is radically different. The era of enthusiasm, unity, mutual understanding, and dedication to a common cause is over. For a long time now I have no longer felt like a bemused plaything of history who is drawn in the same direction as others are, who believes that all are working to the same end as he is, and that they therefore understand him and he need not think too carefully about himself and his program, since "everything is clear". Times have changed, clouds have filled the sky, clarity and general harmony have disappeared, and our country is heading into a period of not inconsiderable difficulties.

The time of hard, everyday work has come, a time in which conflicting interests have surfaced, a time for sobering up, a time when all of us — and especially those in politics — must make it very clear what we stand for.

I too suddenly feel I owe something to my fellow-citizens: a clear, concise account of where I stand, what I actually want, and what I think. True, I have already given hundreds of speeches. Every week I talk to the public on the air. But precisely because my speeches have appeared in so many places (and who, in the rush of events, has had time to follow and take account of them all?), it still seems necessary to me to gather my thoughts, opinions, and intentions together in a single coherent whole.

This book is not a collection of essays, or even less a work of political science. It is merely a series of spontaneously written comments on how I see this country and its problems today, how I see its future, and what I wish to put my efforts behind.

Politics, Morality, and Civility

As RIDICULOUS or quixotic as it may sound these days, one thing seems certain to me: that it is my responsibility to emphasize, again and again, the moral origin of all genuine politics, to stress the significance of moral values and standards in all spheres of social life, including economics, and to explain that if we don't try, within ourselves, to discover or rediscover or cultivate what I call "higher responsibility", things will turn out very badly indeed for our country.

The return of freedom to a society that was morally unhinged has produced something it clearly had to produce, and something we therefore might have expected, but which has turned out to be far more serious than anyone could have predicted: an enormous and dazzling explosion of every imaginable human vice. A wide range of questionable or at least morally ambiguous human tendencies, subtly encouraged over the years and, at the same time, subtly pressed to serve the daily operation of the totalitarian system, have suddenly been liberated, as it were, from their straitjacket and given freedom at last. The authoritarian regime imposed a certain order — if that is the right expression for it — on these vices (and in doing so "legitimized" them, in a sense). This order has now been shattered, but a new order that would limit rather than exploit these vices, an order based on freely accepted responsibility to and for the whole of society, has not yet been built — nor could it have been, for such an order takes years to develop and cultivate.

Thus we are witnesses to a bizarre state of affairs: society has freed itself, true, but in some ways it behaves worse than when it was in chains. Criminality has grown rapidly, and the familiar sewage that in times of historical reversal always wells up from the nether regions of the collective psyche has overflowed into the mass media, especially the gutter press. But there are other, more serious and dangerous symptoms: hatred among nationalities, suspicion, racism, even signs of Fascism; politicking, an unrestrained, unheeding struggle for purely particular interests, unadulterated ambition, fanaticism of every conceivable kind, new and unprecedented varieties of robbery, the rise of different mafias; and a prevailing lack of tolerance, understanding, taste, moderation, and reason. There is a new attraction to ideologies, too — as if Marxism had left behind it a great, disturbing void that had to be filled at any cost.

It is enough to look around our political scene (whose lack of civility is merely a reflection of the more general crisis of civility). In the months leading up to the June 1992 election, almost every political activity, including debates over extremely important legislation in Parliament, has taken place in the shadow of a pre-election campaign, of an extravagant hunger for power and a willingness to gain the favour of a confused electorate by offering a colourful range of attractive nonsense. Mutual accusations, denunciations, and slander among political opponents know no bounds. One politician will undermine another's work only because they belong to different political parties. Partisan considerations still visibly take precedence over pragmatic attempts to arrive at reasonable and useful solutions to problems. Analysis is pushed out of the press by scandalmongering. Supporting the government in a good cause is practically shameful; kicking it in the shins, on the other hand, is praiseworthy. Sniping at politicians who declare their support for another political group is a matter of course. Anyone can accuse anyone else of intrigue or incompetence, or of having a shady past and shady intentions.

Demagogy is rife, and even something as important as the natural longing of a people for autonomy is exploited in power plays, as rivals compete in lying to the public. Many members of the party elite, the so-called *nomenklatura* who, until very recently, were faking concern about social justice and the working class, have cast aside their masks and, almost overnight, openly become speculators and thieves. Many a once-feared Communist is now an unscrupulous capitalist, shamelessly and unequivocally laughing in the face of the same worker whose interests he once allegedly defended.

Citizens are becoming more and more disgusted with all this, and their disgust is understandably directed against the democratic government they themselves elected. Making the most of this situation, some characters with suspicious backgrounds have been gaining popular favour with ideas such as, for instance, the need to throw the entire government into the Vltava River.

And yet, if a handful of friends and I were able to bang our heads against the wall for years by speaking the truth about Communist totalitarianism while surrounded by an ocean of apathy, there is no reason why I shouldn't go on banging my head against the wall by speaking *ad nauseam*, despite the condescending smiles, about responsibility and morality in the face of our present social marasmus. There is no reason to think that this struggle is a lost cause. The only lost cause is one we give up on before we enter the struggle.

TIME and time again I have been persuaded that a huge potential of goodwill is slumbering within our society. It's just that it's incoherent, suppressed, confused, crippled and perplexed — as though it does not know what to rely on, where to begin, where or how to find meaningful outlets.

In such a state of affairs, politicians have a duty to awaken this slumbering potential, to offer it direction and ease its passage, to encourage it and give it room, or simply hope. They say a nation gets the politicians it deserves. In some senses this is true: politicians are indeed a mirror of their society, and a kind of embodiment of its potential. At the same time — paradoxically — the opposite is also true: society is a mirror of its politicians. It is largely up to the politicians which social forces they choose to liberate and which they choose to suppress, whether they rely on the good in each citizen or on the bad. The former regime systematically mobilized the worst human qualities, like selfishness, envy, and hatred. That regime was far more than just something we deserved; it was also responsible for what we became. Those who find themselves in politics therefore bear a heightened responsibility for the moral state of society, and it is their responsibility to seek out the best in that society, and to develop and strengthen it.

By the way, even the politicians who often anger me with their short-sightedness and their malice are not, for the most part, evil-minded. They are, rather, inexperienced, easily infected with the particularisms of the time, easily manipulated by suggestive trends and prevailing customs; often they are simply caught up, unwillingly, in the swirl of bad politics, and find themselves unable to extricate themselves because they are afraid of the risks this would entail.

SOME say I'm a naive dreamer who is always trying to combine the incompatible: politics and morality. I know this song well; I've heard it sung all my life. In the 1980s, a certain Czech philosopher who lived in California published a series of articles in which he subjected the "anti-political politics" of Charter 77 — and, in particular, the way I explained that notion in my essays — to crushing criticism. Trapped in his own Marxist fallacies, he believed that as a scholar he had scientifically comprehended the entire history of the world. He saw it as a history of violent revolutions and vicious power struggles. The idea that the world might actually be changed by the force of truth, the power of a truthful word, the strength of a free spirit, conscience, and responsibility — with no guns, no lust for power, no political wheeling and dealing — was quite beyond the horizon of his understanding. Naturally, if you understand decency as a mere "superstructure" of the forces of production, then you can never understand political power in terms of decency.

Because his doctrine had taught him that the bourgeoisie would never voluntarily surrender its leading role, and that it must be swept into the dustbin of history through armed revolution, this philosopher assumed that there was no other way to sweep away the Communist government either. Yet it turned out to be possible. Moreover, it turned out to be the only way to do it. Not only that, but it was the only way that made sense, since violence, as we know, breeds more violence. This is why most revolutions degenerate into dictatorships that devour their young, giving rise to new revolutionaries who prepare for new violence, unaware that they are digging their own graves and pushing society back onto the deadly merry-go-round of revolution and counter-revolution.

Communism was overthrown by life, by thought, by human dignity. Our recent history has confirmed that the Czech-Californian professor was wrong. Likewise, those who still claim that politics is chiefly the manipulation of power and public opinion, and that morality has no place in it, are just as wrong. Political intrigue is not really politics, and, although you can get away with superficial politics for a time, it does not bring much hope of lasting success. Through intrigue one may easily become prime minister, but that will be the extent of one's success; one can hardly improve the world that way.

I am happy to leave political intrigue to others; I will not compete with them, certainly not by using their weapons.

Genuine politics — politics worthy of the name, and the only politics I am willing to devote myself to — is simply a matter of serving those around us: serving the community, and serving those who will come after us. Its deepest roots are moral because it is a responsibility, expressed through action, to and for the whole, a responsibility that is what it is — a "higher" responsibility — only because it has a metaphysical grounding: that is, it grows out of a conscious or subconscious certainty that our death ends nothing, because everything is forever being recorded and evaluated somewhere else, somewhere "above us", in what I have called "the memory of Being" — an integral aspect of the secret order of the cosmos, of nature, and of life, which believers call God and to whose judgement everything is subject. Genuine conscience and genuine responsibility are always, in the end, explicable only as an expression of the silent assumption that we are observed "from above", that everything is visible, nothing is forgotten, and so earthly time has no power to wipe away the sharp disappointments of earthly failure: our spirit knows that it is not the only entity aware of these failures.

WHAT can I do, as president, not only to remain faithful to that notion of politics, but also to bring it to at least partial fruition? (After all, the former is unthinkable without the latter. Not to put at least some of my ideas into practice could have only two consequences: either I would eventually be swept from office or I would become a tolerated eccentric, sounding off to an unheeding audience — not only a less dignified alternative, but a highly dishonest one as well, because it would mean another form of resignation, both of myself and of my ideals.)

As in everything else, I must start with myself. That is: in all circumstances try to be decent, just, tolerant, and understanding, and at the same time try to resist corruption and deception. In other words, I must do my utmost to act in harmony with my conscience and my better self. For instance, I am frequently advised to be more "tactical", not to say everything right away, to dissimulate gently, not to fear wooing someone more than my nature commands, or to distance myself from someone against my real will in the matter. In the interests of strengthening my hand, I am advised at times to assent to someone's ambition for power, to flatter someone merely because it pleases him, or to reject someone even though it goes against my convictions, because he does not enjoy favour with others.

I constantly hear another kind of advice, as well: I should be tougher, more decisive, more authoritative. For a good cause, I shouldn't be afraid to pound the table occasionally, to shout at people, to try to rouse a little fear and trembling. Yet, if I wish to remain faithful to myself and my notion of politics, I mustn't listen to advice like this — not just in the interests of my personal mental health (which could be seen as a private, selfish desire), but chiefly in the interests of what most concerns me: the simple fact that directness can never be established by indirection, or truth through lies, or the democratic spirit through authoritarian directives. Of course, I don't know whether directness, truth, and the democratic spirit will succeed. But I do know how *not* to succeed, which is by choosing means that contradict the ends. As we know from history, that is the best way to eliminate the very ends we set out to achieve.

In other words, if there is to be any chance at all of success, there is only one way to strive for decency, reason, responsibility, sincerity, civility, and tolerance, and that is decently, reasonably, responsibly, sincerely, civilly, and tolerantly. I'm aware that, in everyday politics, this is not seen as the most practical way of going about it. But I have one advantage: among my many bad qualities there is one that happens to be missing — a longing or a love for power. Not being bound by that, I am essentially freer than those who cling to their power or position, and this allows me to indulge in the luxury of behaving untactically.

I see the only way forward in that old, familiar injunction: "live in truth".

But how is this to be done, practically speaking, when one is president? I see three basic possibilities.

The first possibility: I must repeat certain things aloud over and over again. I don't like repeating myself, but in this case it's unavoidable. In my many public utterances, I feel I must emphasize and explain repeatedly the moral dimensions of all social life, and point out that morality is, in fact, hidden in everything. And this is true: whenever I encounter a problem in my work and try to get to the bottom of it, I always discover some moral aspect, be it apathy, unwillingness to recognize personal error or guilt, reluctance to give up certain positions and the advantages flowing from them, envy, an excess of self-assurance, or whatever.

I feel that the dormant goodwill in people needs to be stirred. People need to hear that it makes sense to behave decently or to help others, to place common interests above their own, to respect the elementary rules of human coexistence. They want to be told about this publicly. They want to know that those "at the top" are on their side. They feel strengthened, confirmed, hopeful. Goodwill longs to be recognized and cultivated. For it to develop and have an impact it must hear that the world does not ridicule it.

Frequently, regular listeners to my radio talks to the nation, "Conversations from Lány", ask to hear what might be called "philosophical" or "ethical" reflections. I occasionally omit them for fear of repeating myself too often, but people always ask for them again. I try never to give people practical advice about how to deal with the evil around them, nor could I even if I wanted to — and yet people want to hear that decency and courage make sense, that something must be risked in the struggle against dirty tricks. They want to know they are not alone, forgotten, written off.

The second possibility: I can try to create around me, in the world of so-called high politics, a positive climate, a climate of generosity, tolerance, openness, broadmindedness, and a kind of elementary companionship and mutual trust. In this sphere I am far from being the decisive factor. But I can have a psychological influence.

The third possibility: There is a significant area in which I do have direct political influence in my position as president. I am required to make certain political decisions. In this, I can and must bring my concept of politics to bear, and inject into it my political ideals, my longing for justice, decency, and civility, my notion of what, for present purposes, I will call "the moral state". Whether I am successful or not is for others to judge, of course, but the results will always be uneven, since, like everyone else, I am a fallible human being.

JOURNALISTS, and in particular foreign correspondents, often ask me how the idea of "living in truth", the idea of "anti-political politics", or the idea of politics subordinated to conscience can, in practice, be carried out. They are curious to know whether, finding myself in high office, I have not had to revise much of what I once wrote as an independent critic of politics and politicians. Have I not been compelled to lower my former "dissident" expectations of politics, by which they mean the standards I derived from the "dissident experience", which are therefore scarcely applicable outside that sphere?

There may be some who won't believe me, but in my second term as president in a land full of problems that presidents in stable countries never even dream of, I can safely say that I have not been compelled to recant anything of what I wrote earlier, or to change my mind about anything. It may seem incredible, but it is so: not only have I not had to change my mind, but my opinions have been confirmed.

Despite the political distress I face every day, I am still deeply convinced that politics is not essentially a disreputable business; and to the extent that it is, it is only disreputable people who make it so. I would concede that it can, more than other spheres of human activity, tempt one to disreputable practices, and that it therefore places higher demands on people. But it is simply not true that a politician must lie or intrigue. That is utter nonsense, spread about by people who — for whatever reasons — wish to discourage others from taking an interest in public affairs.

Of course, in politics, as elsewhere in life, it is impossible and pointless to say everything, all at once, to just anyone. But that does not mean having to lie. All you need is tact, the proper instincts, and good taste. One surprising experience from "high politics" is this: I have discovered that good taste is more useful here than a post-graduate degree in political science. It is largely a matter of form: knowing how long to speak, when to begin and when to finish; how to say something politely that your opposite number may not want to hear; how to say, always, what is most significant at a given moment, and not to speak of what is not important or relevant; how to insist on your own position without offending; how to create the kind of friendly atmosphere that makes complex negotiations easier; how to keep a conversation going without prying or being aloof; how to balance serious political themes with lighter, more relaxing topics; how to plan your official journeys judiciously and to know when it is more appropriate not to go somewhere, when to be open and when reticent and to what degree.

But more than that, it means having a certain instinct for the time, the atmosphere of the time, the mood of people, the nature of their worries, their frame of mind — that too can perhaps be more useful than sociological surveys. An education in political science, law, economics, history, and culture is an invaluable asset to any politician, but I have been persuaded, again and again, that it is not the most essential asset. Qualities like fellow-feeling, the ability to talk to others, insight, the capacity to grasp quickly not only problems but also human character, the ability to make contact, a sense of moderation: all these are immensely more important in politics. I am not saying, heaven forbid, that I myself am endowed with these qualities; not at all! These are merely my observations.

To sum up: if your heart is in the right place and you have good taste, not only will you pass muster in politics, you are destined for it. If you are modest and do not lust after power, not only are you suited to politics, you absolutely belong there. The *sine qua non* of a politician is not the ability to lie; he need only be sensitive and know when, what, to whom, and how to say what he has to say. It is not true that a person of principle does not belong in politics; it is enough for his principles to be leavened with patience, deliberation, a sense of proportion, and an understanding of others. It is not true that only the unfeeling cynic, the vain, the brash, and the vulgar can succeed in politics; such people, it is true, are drawn to politics, but, in the end, decorum and good taste will always count for more.

My experience and observations confirm that politics as the practice of morality is possible. I do not deny, however, that it is not always easy to go that route, nor have I ever claimed that it was.

FROM my political ideals, it should be clear enough that what I would like to accentuate in every possible way in my practice of politics is culture. Culture in the widest possible sense of the word, including everything from what might be called the culture of everyday life — or "civility" — to what we know as high culture, including the arts and sciences.

I don't mean that the state should heavily subsidize culture as a particular area of human endeavour, nor do I at all share the indignant fear of many artists that the period we are going through now is ruining culture and will eventually destroy it. Most of our artists have, unwittingly, grown accustomed to the unending generosity of the socialist state. It subsidized a number of cultural institutions and offices, heedless of whether a film cost one million or ten million crowns, or whether anyone ever went to see it.

It didn't matter how many idle actors the theatres had on their payrolls; the main thing was that everyone was on one, and thus on the take. The Communist state knew, better than the Czech-Californian philosopher, where the greatest danger to it lay: in the realm of the intellect and the spirit. It knew who first had to be pacified through irrational largesse. That the state was less and less successful at doing so is another matter, which merely confirms how right it was to be afraid; for, despite all the bribes and prizes and titles thrown their way, the artists were among the first to rebel.

This nostalgic complaint by artists who fondly remember their "social security" under socialism therefore leaves me unmoved. Culture must, in part at least, learn how to make its own way. It should be partially funded through tax write-offs, and through foundations, development funds, and the like — which, by the way, are the forms that best suit its plurality and its freedom. The more varied the sources of funding for the arts and sciences, the greater variety and competition there will be in the arts and in scholarly research. The state should — in ways that are rational, open to scrutiny, and well thought out — support only those aspects of culture that are fundamental to our national identity and the civilized traditions of our land, and that can't be conserved through market mechanisms alone. I am thinking of heritage sites (there can't be a hotel in every castle or château to pay for its upkeep, nor can the old aristocracy be expected to return and provide for their upkeep merely to preserve family honour), libraries, museums, public archives, and such institutions, which today are in an appalling state of disrepair (as though the previous "regime of forgetting" deliberately set out to destroy these important witnesses to our past). Likewise, it is hard to imagine that the Church, or the churches, in the foreseeable future, will have the means to restore all the chapels, cathedrals, monasteries, and ecclesiastical buildings that have fallen into ruin over the forty years of Communism. They are part of the cultural wealth of the entire country, not just the pride of the Church.

I mention all this only by way of introduction, for the sake of exactness. My main point is something else. I consider it immensely important that we concern ourselves with culture not just as one among many human activities, but in the broadest sense — the "culture of everything", the general level of public manners. By that I mean chiefly the kind of relations that exist among people, between the powerful and the weak, the healthy and the sick, the young and the elderly, adults and children, businesspeople and customers, men and women, teachers and students, officers and soldiers, policemen and citizens, and so on.

More than that, I am also thinking of the quality of people's relationships to nature, to animals, to the atmosphere, to the landscape, to towns, to gardens, to their homes — the culture of housing and architecture, of public catering, of big business and small shops; the culture of work and advertising; the culture of fashion, behaviour, and entertainment.

And there is even more: all this would be hard to imagine without a legal, political, and administrative culture, without the culture of relationships between the state and the citizen. Before the war, in all these areas, we were on the same level as the prosperous western democracies of the day, if not higher. To assess our present condition, it's enough to cross into Western Europe. I know that this catastrophic decline in the general cultural level, the level of public manners, is related to the decline in our economy, and is even, to a large degree, a direct consequence of it. Still, it frightens me more than economic decline does. It is more visible; it impinges on one more "physically", as it were. I can well imagine that, as a citizen, it would bother me more if the pub I went to were a place where the customers spat on the floor and the staff behaved boorishly towards me than it would if I could no longer afford to go there every day and order the most expensive meal on the menu. Likewise, it would bother me less not to be able to afford a family house than it would not to see nice houses anywhere.

Perhaps what I'm trying to say is clear: however important it may be to get our economy back on its feet, it is far from being the only task facing us. It is no less important to do everything possible to improve the general cultural level of everyday life. As the economy develops, this will happen anyway. But we cannot depend on that alone. We must initiate a large-scale program for raising general cultural standards. And it is not true that we have to wait until we are rich to do this; we can begin at once, without a crown in our pockets. No one can persuade me that it takes a better-paid nurse to behave more considerately to a patient, that only an expensive house can be pleasing, that only a wealthy merchant can be courteous to his customers and display a handsome sign outside, that only a prosperous farmer can treat his livestock well. I would go even farther, and say that, in many respects, improving the civility of everyday life can accelerate economic development — from the culture of supply and demand, of trading and enterprise, right down to the culture of values and lifestyle.

I want to do everything I can to contribute, in a specific way, to a program for raising the general level of civility, or at least do everything I can to express my personal interest in such an improvement, whether I do so as president or not. I feel this is both an integral part and a logical consequence of my notion of politics as the practice of morality and the application of a "higher responsibility". After all, is there anything that citizens — and this is doubly true of politicians — should be more concerned about, ultimately, than trying to make life more pleasant, more interesting, more varied, and more bearable?

IF I TALK here about my political — or, more precisely, my civil — program, about my notion of the kind of politics and values and ideals I wish to struggle for, this is not to say that I am entertaining the naive hope that this struggle may one day be over. A heaven on earth in which people all love each other and everyone is hard-working, well-mannered, and virtuous, in which the land flourishes and everything is sweetness and light, working harmoniously to the satisfaction of God: this will never be. On the contrary, the world has had the worst experiences with utopian thinkers who promised all that. Evil will remain with us, no one will ever eliminate human suffering, the political arena will always attract irresponsible and ambitious adventurers and charlatans. And man will not stop destroying the world. In this regard, I have no illusions.

Neither I nor anyone else will ever win this war once and for all. At the very most, we can win a battle or two — and not even that is certain. Yet I still think it makes sense to wage this war persistently. It has been waged for centuries, and it will continue to be waged — we hope — for centuries to come. This must be done on principle, because it is the right thing to do. Or, if you like, because God wants it that way. It is an eternal, never-ending struggle waged not just by good people (among whom I count myself, more or less) against evil people, by honourable people against dishonourable people, by people who think about the world and eternity against people who think only of themselves and the moment. It takes place inside everyone. It is what makes a person a person, and life, life.

So anyone who claims that I am a dreamer who expects to transform hell into heaven is wrong. I have few illusions. But I feel a responsibility to work towards the things I consider good and right. I don't know whether I'll be able to change certain things for the better, or not at all. Both outcomes are possible. There is only one thing I will not concede: that it might be meaningless to strive in a good cause.

WE ARE building our country anew. Fate has thrust me into a position in which I have a somewhat greater influence on that process than most of my fellow citizens do. It is appropriate, therefore, that I admit to my notions about what kind of country it should be, and articulate the vision that guides me — or rather, the vision that flows naturally from politics as I understand it.

Perhaps we can all agree that we want a state based on rule of law, one that is democratic (that is, with a pluralistic political system), peaceful, and with a prospering market economy. Some insist that this state should also be socially just. Others sense in the phrase a hangover from socialism and argue against it. They object to the notion of "social justice" as vague, claiming that it can mean anything at all, and that a functioning market economy can never guarantee any genuine social justice. They point out that people have, and always will have, different degrees of industriousness, talent, and, last but not least, luck. Obviously, social justice in the sense of social equality is something the market system cannot, by its very nature, deliver. Moreover, to compel the marketplace to do so would be deeply immoral. (Our experience of socialism has provided us with more than enough examples of why this is so.)

I do not see, however, why a democratic state, armed with a legislature and the power to draw up a budget, cannot strive for a certain fairness in, for example, pension policies or tax policies, or support to the unemployed, or salaries to public employees, or assistance to the elderly living alone, people who have health problems, or those who, for various reasons, find themselves at the bottom of society. Every civilized state attempts, in different ways and with different degrees of success, to come up with reasonable policies in these areas, and not even the most ardent supporters of the market economy have anything against it in principle. In the end, then, it is a conflict not of beliefs, but rather of terminology.

I am repeating these basic, self-evident, and rather general facts for the sake of completeness and order. But I would like to say more about other aspects of the state that may be somewhat less obvious and are certainly much less talked about, but are no less important — because they qualify and make possible everything that is considered self-evident.

I am convinced that we will never build a democratic state based on rule of law if we do not at the same time build a state that is — regardless of how unscientific this may sound to the ears of a political scientist — humane, moral, intellectual and spiritual, and cultural. The best laws and the best-conceived democratic mechanisms will not in themselves guarantee legality or freedom or human rights — anything, in short, for which they were intended — if they are not underpinned by certain human and social values. What good, for instance, would a law be if no one respected it, no one defended it, and no one tried responsibly to follow it? It would be nothing but a scrap of paper. What use would elections be in which the voter's only choice was between a greater and a lesser scoundrel? What use would a wide variety of political parties be if not one of them had the general interest of society at heart?

No state — that is, no constitutional, legal, and political

system — is anything in and of itself, outside historical time and social space. It is not the clever technical invention of a team of experts, like a computer or a telephone. Every state, on the contrary, grows out of specific intellectual, spiritual, and cultural traditions that breathe substance into it and give it meaning.

So we are back to the same point: without commonly shared and widely entrenched moral values and obligations, neither the law, nor democratic government, nor even the market economy will function properly. They are all marvellous products of the human spirit, mechanisms that can, in turn, serve the spirit magnificently — assuming that the human spirit wants these mechanisms to serve it, respects them, believes in them, guarantees them, understands their meaning, and is willing, if necessary, to fight for them or make sacrifices for them.

Again I would use law as an illustration. The law is undoubtedly an instrument of justice, but it would be an utterly meaningless instrument if no one used it responsibly. From our own recent experience we all know too well what can happen to even a decent law in the hands of an unscrupulous judge, and how easily unscrupulous people can use democratic institutions to introduce dictatorship and terror. The law and other democratic institutions ensure little if they are not backed up by the willingness and courage of decent people to guard against their abuse. That these institutions can help us become more human is obvious; that is why they were created, and why we are building them now. But if they are to guarantee anything to us, it is we, first of all, who must guarantee them.

In the somewhat chaotic provisional activity around the technical aspects of building the state, it will do us no harm occasionally to remind ourselves of the meaning of the state, which is, and must remain, truly human — which means it must be intellectual, spiritual, and moral.

HOW ARE we to go about building such a state? What does such an ambition bind us to or offer us, in practical terms?

There is no simple set of instructions on how to proceed. A moral and intellectual state cannot be established through a constitution, or through law, or through directives, but only through complex, long-term, and never-ending work involving education and self-education. What is needed is lively and responsible consideration of every political step, every decision; a constant stress on moral deliberation and moral judgement; continued self-examination and self-analysis; an endless rethinking of our priorities. It is not, in short, something we can simply declare or introduce. It is a way of going about things, and it demands the courage to breathe moral and spiritual motivation into everything, to seek the human dimension in all things. Science, technology, expertise, and so-called professionalism are not enough. Something more is necessary. For the sake of simplicity, it might be called spirit. Or feeling. Or conscience.

In a Time of
Transition

IN JUNE 1990, our three parliaments — the federal and
the two republican parliaments — were elected with a
two-year mandate. Shortly after that the Federal Assembly
re-elected me president of the republic for the same two-
year mandate.

Many western politicians were surprised that we decided
on such a short time between elections. They argued that
all kinds of good things may be set in motion in the course
of two years, but almost nothing can be brought to a proper
conclusion.

I confess I was one of the main proponents of this drastically brief mandate. My reasoning was this: we found ourselves in a transitional period, when everything — from a
constitutional and legal system to a pluralistic political
spectrum — was, in fact, being reborn. Everything was
provisional, and much of what we did was an improvised
search for solutions. Such a situation required that we work
quickly, for any prolongation of this ill-defined and transi-
tory state could only have unfortunate consequences.

The main task of Parliament was to approve a new constitution. Having a two-year mandate compelled Parliament
to work quickly, and the cornerstone of our democratic
state thus stood a good chance of being carved out and laid
within those two years. If Parliament had had four years,
the same work would almost certainly have taken four years,
without the results necessarily having been any better for
it. On the contrary, my fear was that they might have been

worse. The provisional state of affairs would have been extended to an untenable length. It is hard to live for long in a state of uncertainty; society would have found it difficult to bear, and calls for early elections, for whatever reason, would have come with increasing frequency.

Moreover, the elections of June 1990 were not really elections in the true and traditional sense of the word; they were more like a popular referendum. The idea of democracy won in every respect, but the outcome was not yet a genuine, fully fledged democracy. The election results could not reflect the real political stratification of society because that stratification was just beginning to take shape, and because, at the time, there did not yet exist, nor could there exist, a comprehensible and stable spectrum of distinct political parties. It was clear that during the next two years or so this spectrum would begin to materialize (which has in fact happened), and that by the time the two years were up the situation would be sufficiently clear and the time ripe enough to make proper elections possible — elections as they are understood in mature democracies. Citizens would be able to exercise their franchise in the "pure" sense of the word: they would vote according to a new constitution, they would send representatives to new and better-structured assemblies, and they would have a better idea — thanks to the transitional two-year "trial" phase — of what each party actually wanted and who now belonged to the parties.

The 1990 elections were, to a considerable extent, the last echo, or rather the culmination, of our revolution, and so they necessarily exhibited many revolutionary qualities (once I even called them a "dress rehearsal" for real elections). But the June 1992 elections should mark the beginning of a calmer and more stable era, one founded on a new, more rational, and truly democratic constitutional and political system. To drag out the "revolutionary" phase, to prolong some of the improvisational measures (including the absurd business of gluing amendments and addenda to the Communist constitution), to delay the creation of something as basic as a new constitution, could have fatal consequences for our nascent democracy. An extended period of uncertainty and confusion leads only to a state of general anarchy and frustration, and a permanent social crisis. If I have had some clear successes during my term of office, it has always been because I acted swiftly when the occasion called for it. Many failures and crises could have been avoided had we hesitated less and not put some things off until later. Let one example stand for all: there would have been no need whatever to go through such a prolonged struggle over the name of our country had we simply made a slight break with parliamentary tradition and dropped the word "socialist" from the name "Czechoslovak Socialist Republic" the very same day I made the proposal to Parliament, instead of becoming sidetracked by arguments like "We need time to consider it." Other post-Communist countries have dealt with that question in an hour.

It is almost certain that we will not have succeeded in clarifying the future organization of our state and passing the new constitution by the 1992 elections. When I recall the dozens and dozens of hours I have spent over the past year in meetings about the constitution, the thought that these negotiations may drag on to, say, 1994 makes me cringe in dismay. Four years of wrangling about the future shape of our country could well mean that, at the end of the day, we will not have a country to organize and give a new constitutional order to. To this day, therefore, I do not regret that we set ourselves the target of only two years to carry out some of our basic tasks.

Some people, by the way, suggested that the president, at least — as a guarantor of continuity — should have been elected for a longer term. I was vehemently against that as well, and finally got my way. I had several reasons, the main one being that a country with a new constitution, and with a president whose powers and means of election might quite possibly be defined differently, should not have to inherit a president left over from the previous era, elected according to the old constitution. Also, I felt our chances of bringing about the required changes would be greater if all those involved in making them were bound by the same term of office.

In almost all the post-Communist countries, elections have been held earlier than originally planned, or more often than is common in stable democracies. This is related to the dynamics of the changes, to the speed of the political developments — and to the fact that time flies faster in this part of the world. And it is certainly better to plan for early elections than to let the dramatic course of events impose premature elections upon us.

TO SOME it may seem that I am attaching more importance to the creation and ratification of a new constitution than the process warrants. I understand this entirely. After all, for decades it made no difference whatsoever what our constitution called for; it had no effect on the everyday life of the citizen, it had nothing to do with how we lived, or whether the Communists took a hard line or permitted a thaw. The Communist Party ran everything anyway, and it was no problem for them to arrange things so that their dictatorship was always in compliance with the constitution. I can understand that, against the background of this long experience, many people even today may see a constitution as something highly theoretical, abstract, out of touch with reality, of interest to politicians but with no direct effect on their own lives. What is more important to people is whether the cost of living is high, whether their jobs are secure, whether the company they work for is intelligently run and prosperous or run by a mafia interested only in lining its own pockets.

I understand such sentiments, but I also know they are wrong. Every day I am persuaded that in our situation almost everything depends on the nascent constitutional system — or is at least related to it in some way: whether we will be a single country or two separate countries, one Czech and one Slovak; how the economic reforms will proceed; what kind of people will lead our country and what powers they will have; what influence citizens will have on how they are governed.

Take, for example, the question of division of powers, whether it be between the federal government and the two republican governments, or between the local administrations or companies and the ministries and different elements of the executive branch of government. Nothing in a citizen's everyday life is unaffected by this. Even the question of whether the trains run or how much tickets cost depends to a considerable degree on which directorate or ministry runs them, or which institution is vying for their control.

There's no way around it: the rule of law is back. And so it is once more important what kind of laws we have. And this depends above all on the constitution, from which all laws are derived. I would even go so far as to say that our everyday lives depend as much on the kind of constitution we have as they do on the kind of country we live in. After all, it is becoming true once again that the constitution is what defines our state.

That is why, soon after I was re-elected president, I set as one of my priorities — if not my top priority — the preparation of a new federal constitution. That is why I convoked a long series of political discussions on the theme. That is also why, in early 1991, I made my own working draft of a federal constitution available for public discussion.

THE BASIC question around which the drafting of a federal constitution revolves today — and the one that is also the major impediment to it — is what constitutional form our country will adopt, or, more precisely, what relationship will exist between the two peoples — the Czechs and the Slovaks — and the two republics that now form the federation.

Everything indicates that most Czechs had no idea how strong was the longing of the Slovaks for autonomy and for their own constitutional expression, and that they were more than surprised at how quickly after our democratic revolution this longing began to stir, and how powerfully it expressed itself.

When I think about this phenomenon — which seems purely irrational to many Czechs, and even a betrayal of the Czech nation and the Czechoslovak state — I find that I do understand one aspect of it very well, certainly whenever I spend time in Slovakia: the aversion the Slovaks feel to being governed from elsewhere. Throughout their history — with the single infamous exception of the Slovak State, granted its independence by Hitler in 1938 — they have always been ruled from elsewhere. And as they became more aware of their national identity, this began to bother them increasingly. For almost as long as the Czechoslovak state has existed, they have, *de facto*, been ruled from Prague — and they are acutely aware of that. For many Slovaks, whether they are governed well or badly, with their participation or without it, with their interests in mind or without them, is less important than the bare fact that they are governed from somewhere else.

It should be no surprise, therefore, that whenever the

situation in Czechoslovakia becomes the slightest bit fluid, the Slovaks always try in some way appropriate to the moment to disengage themselves from Prague. This disengagement has always appeared to be, in itself, more important to them than its political context. I still have vivid memories of how, during the Prague Spring of 1968, some Slovak intellectuals coined the slogan "First federalization, then democratization" — without understanding that there can be no genuine federation without democracy. And sure enough, when the Soviet invasion ended the Prague Spring, the Slovaks were granted federalization — but what they got was totalitarian federalization. (The paradox is that what was in 1968 the slogan of the day and the aim of everyone in Slovakia — federalization — is now used by a significant number of Slovak political representatives, and the Slovak press, as though it were a synonym for "Prague centralism". The alien word "federal" has come, in Slovakia, to mean the same as "oppressor". And the notion of a federation is perceived as almost a Czech invention and a Czech con game, aimed at limiting Slovak autonomy.)

The Slovak nation is smaller than the Czech nation. For centuries, it has never had its own state, as the Czechs have had. For a long time, Slovak society was not as stratified or as complex as Czech society. Its historical experience, its models of social behaviour, and its way of life have all been different, though this is not often noticed by Czechs. This means that since the birth of our common Czechoslovak state in 1918, regardless of the specific political conditions pertaining and the specific policies applied by the "centre", the Slovaks have always felt that they were an overlooked and forgotten smaller and weaker brother, condemned to live in the bigger and stronger brother's shadow. From the sociological or political point of view, the justness of such feelings is not important. What matters is that such feelings existed, and continue to exist. In any case, the various attempts by the central authorities — whether it was the so-called Czechoslovakian unitary state or, ultimately, the federal state — to contribute to the rapid development of Slovakia inevitably turned many Slovaks against the Czechs, all the more so because some of these attempts, especially during the Communist era, were highly dubious. Anyone who can't understand this should read J. William Fulbright's book *The Arrogance of Power*, in which the author explains why Americans are often hated in countries they have tried to help. It is instructive reading, not only for Slovaks but — even more so, perhaps — for Czechs.

Though it may seem like it at times, the issue in Slovakia is not essentially an aversion to Czechs as such but an aversion to the fact that the centre of power over Slovakia is somewhere outside its territory — and is, moreover, on the territory of its bigger and older and richer brother. This feeling is so deep and so powerful that it can scarcely be countered by facts or down-to-earth arguments. The central government offices and ministries in Prague could be filled with Slovaks, yet that would do nothing to change Slovak attitudes. Slovak politicians in Prague are often seen as renegades, sometimes even as turncoats and sell-outs, and certainly as "less authentic" Slovaks — and this despite their having fought vehemently for their seats in Prague in the name of Slovak interests.

This Slovak attitude, which would probably be the same whether the seat of central power were in Prague, Budapest, Warsaw, or Brussels, is something I understand completely. Even if the Czechoslovak federation survives, even if it is genuinely just and, over time, gains the confidence and trust of Slovaks, Slovakia will still find it hard to accept that its capital city is Prague and that fundamental decisions affecting it are therefore made outside Slovakia. I am afraid that even if some of the federal institutions were to move to Bratislava, the capital of Slovakia, the deeply rooted bitterness would persist, for this would most probably be interpreted as a mere gesture on Prague's part, a sop to the Slovaks, changing nothing essential in the dominant position of Prague.

The Slovaks do not aspire to govern the Czechs. They see themselves as a completely autonomous community that wishes to make decisions about its own affairs at home. Such a will to autonomy is, of course, entirely legitimate, and nothing can change that — not even the primitive, xenophobic, and suicidal nationalism that frequently accompanies it. All nations must go through a phase of national self-awareness and, related to that, a phase of struggle for a state of their own, and they must experience national sovereignty before they can mature to the point of realizing that membership in supranational bodies based on the notion of a civil society not only does not suppress their national identity and sovereignty, but in a sense extends it, strengthens it, and nurtures it.

In this regard the Czechs are, it would seem, farther along than the Slovaks, not because they are by nature more advanced, but solely because they have a somewhat different history, part of which is that they have always perceived Czechoslovakia — far more than the Slovaks ever did — as their own country. At times they were so selfish, disparaging, and insensitive about it that they drove the Slovaks to stop thinking of Czechoslovakia as *their* country. (This is why the idea of Czech statehood — which people are talking about more frequently today, as a reaction to the rise of Slovak nationalism — has very little resonance in the Czech lands of Bohemia and Moravia so far; so completely is the idea of Czech statehood identified in people's minds with the idea of Czechoslovak statehood that to many a separate Czech state makes no sense at all.)

I think the Slovak will to emancipation is an integral part of the present historical moment in Central and Eastern

Europe. In their modern history, the nations here — unlike the nations of Western Europe — have had very little opportunity to taste fully the delights of statehood. They have always been the subjects of someone else, and most recently their autonomy was repressed by the straitjacket of Communism and Soviet hegemony. They are merely trying to make up for lost time, and everything must be done to allow them to go through this phase — in which such exaggerated stress is placed on all things national — as quickly and in as civilized a manner as possible. Both in their own and in the general interest, they must be allowed to catch up with countries with a happier history.

PERHAPS it would be appropriate at this point for me to talk briefly about how I see the so-called national principle.

The category of home belongs in the category of what modern philosophers call the "natural world". (The Czech philosopher Jan Patočka analysed this notion before the Second World War.) For everyone, home is a basic existential experience. What a person perceives as home (in the philosophical sense of the word) can be compared to a set of concentric circles, with one's "I" at the centre. My home is the room I live in for a time, the room I've grown accustomed to and have, in a manner of speaking, covered with my own invisible lining. I recall, for instance, that even my prison cell was my home in a sense, and I felt very put out whenever I was suddenly required to move to another. The new cell may have been exactly the same as the old one, perhaps even better, but I always experienced it as alien and unfriendly. I felt uprooted and surrounded by strangeness, and it would take me some time to get used to it, to stop missing the previous cell, to make myself at home.

My home is the house I live in, the village or town where I was born or where I spend most of my time. My home is my family, the world of my friends, my profession, my company, my workplace. My home, obviously, is also the country I live in, and its intellectual and spiritual climate, expressed in the language spoken there. The Czech language, the Czech way of perceiving the world, the Czech historical experience, the Czech modes of courage and cowardice, Czech humour — all of these are inseparable from that circle of my home. My home is therefore my Czechness, my nationality, and I see no reason at all why I shouldn't embrace it since it is as essential a part of me as, say, my masculinity, another stratum of my home. My home is not only my Czechness, of course; it is also my Czechoslovakness, which means my citizenship. Beyond that, my home is Europe and my Europeanness and — ultimately — it is this world and its present civilization and for that matter the universe.

But that is not all: my home is also my education, my upbringing, my habits, my social milieu. And if I belonged to a political party, that would indisputably be my home as well.

Every circle, every aspect of the human home, has to be given its due. It makes no sense to deny or forcibly exclude any one stratum for the sake of another; none should be regarded as less important or inferior. They are part of our natural world, and a properly organized society has to respect them all and give them all the chance to play their roles. This is the only way that room can be made for people to realize themselves freely as human beings, to exercise their identities. All the circles of our home, indeed our whole natural world, are an inalienable part of us, and an inseparable element of our human identity. Deprived of all the aspects of his home, man would be deprived of himself, of his humanity.

I favour a political system based on the citizen and recognizing all fundamental civil and human rights in their universal validity, equally applied; that is, no member of a single race, a single nation, a single sex, or a single religion may be endowed with basic rights that are any different from anyone else's. In other words, I favour what is called a civil society.

Today, this principle is sometimes presented as if it were opposed to the principle of national affiliation, as if it ignored or suppressed the stratum of our home represented by our nationality. This is a crude misunderstanding. On the contrary, the principle of civil society represents the best way for individuals to realize themselves, to fulfil their identity in all the circles of their home, to enjoy everything that belongs to their natural world, not just some aspects of it. To establish a state on any other basis — on the principle of ideology, or nationality, or religion, for instance — means making a single stratum of our home superior to the others, and thus detracting from us as people, and detracting from our natural world. The outcome is almost always bad. Most wars and revolutions, for example, come about precisely because of this one-dimensional concept of the state. A state based on citizenship, one that respects people and all levels of their natural world, will be a basically peaceable and humane state.

I certainly do not want to suppress the national dimension of a person's identity, or deny it, or refuse to acknowledge its legitimacy and its right to full self-realization. I merely reject the kind of political notions that, in the name of nationality, attempt to suppress other aspects of the human home, other aspects of humanity and human rights. And it seems to me that a civil society, based on the universality of human rights, can best allow us to realize ourselves as everything we are — not only members of our nation, but members of our family, our community, our region, our church, our professional association, our political party, our country, our supranational communities — because it treats us chiefly as human beings whose individuality finds its primary, most natural, and most universal expression in citizenship, in the broadest and deepest sense of that word.

The sovereignty of the community, the region, the nation, the state — any higher sovereignty, in fact — makes sense only if it is derived from the one genuine sovereignty — that is, from the sovereignty of the human being, which finds its political expression in civil sovereignty.

BUT BACK to Slovakia.

I don't think full statehood would bring anything good to Slovakia. The historical euphoria that newly gained independence would bring, and the pride at having their own state, would not last long, and would soon be followed — as a consequence of the hard realities of independence — by a period of sobering up.

Still, I think the decision is entirely up to Slovakia. The right of a nation to govern itself and not share with anyone the power over its own affairs is inalienable and must be respected. That is why, in December 1990, I proposed that the Federal Assembly pass a constitutional law authorizing a referendum to determine whether Czechs and Slovaks want to go on living together in a common country. I don't think such serious matters should be left up to the representative legislative bodies alone, no matter how democratically they were elected. The people themselves should decide. I was delighted when the Federal Assembly finally passed the law in July 1991, and I continue to support efforts to hold a state-wide referendum. Nevertheless, events since then have placed the referendum in jeopardy, and it will not likely happen before the election in June. The problem is that my proposal was accepted but in an incomplete form, such that it is now impossible to declare a referendum if Parliament can't come to an agreement on the wording of the question. The whole point of a referendum is that, if Parliament can't agree on something, the voters are given a chance to decide. But if Parliament can't agree on an issue, it obviously won't be able to agree on the wording of a referendum either. That is why, in an amendment I tabled in Parliament last fall, I proposed that neither the wording of the question nor the power to declare a referendum be exclusively in Parliament's hands. This too was rejected, and it is no longer clear what form the principle of a referendum will take in any new constitution.

For the time being, however, the referendum law is a constitutional law — that is to say, it is part of our constitution. The results of the referendum will therefore — as the law states — be as binding as a constitutional law. I will respect the results of that referendum, not despite my oath, but precisely because I have given my word.

Anyone in Slovakia who describes me as an enemy of the Slovak nation, a new oppressor who desires — either by violence or by some clever political chicanery — to rob it once more of its freedom, is lying to his own nation and thereby harming it. I took an oath to defend the constitution of our common state. To me, this does not mean forcing federation on a nation that does not want to live within it. It merely means that my duty is to defend the law and the constitution.

WHAT I think myself, however — what I favour, and what I personally consider right and proper — is another matter.

Here too I must be clear: I am unequivocally in favour of the federal state, and I would consider its eventual collapse a grave misfortune for all Czechoslovak citizens.

From time immemorial our two nations have been bound together by thousands of historical, cultural, and personal ties. Our forefathers freely elected to live in a common

Czech and Slovak state and they had good reasons for doing so. If we were to go our separate ways now, it would be a rejection of the will of whole generations, a rejection of the common achievement of our Slovak and Czech forebears, a rejection of the ideals that brought about our common state. This, however, does nothing to change the fact that at different times in our history this country has, for various reasons, betrayed the ideals and agreements that prepared the way for its creation.

The responsibility we bear now goes beyond this moment. It is not just a responsibility to our contemporaries, but to those who came before us and, above all, to those who will come after us. I am deeply persuaded that, if we were to separate today, future generations would see it as a fatal error, and would never forgive us.

The disintegration of Czechoslovakia would also have fatal consequences for us. It is worth reminding ourselves of some of them.

In the first place: a state is a state if it is a subject of international law — that is, if it is recognized as an independent state by the world community. Czechoslovakia has been such a state since 1918 (not counting the intermezzo of the Second World War), and its existence and the validity of its borders are guaranteed by a number of international treaties. If the country were to divide, this complex and elaborately constructed fabric — the work of decades — would immediately unravel and it would be a long time indeed before it was replaced by something new.

The demise of this set of agreements would have serious economic consequences as well. All the international economic agreements and all the relationships flowing from them would be disrupted. Our somewhat uncertain position in the world economic environment would become even more questionable than it already is. Outside interest in loans, lines of credit, investment, trade, and our products would rapidly decline, because we would suddenly become an unknown quantity. Our identity would remain unclear throughout the whole painful period when state assets and liabilities were being divided. Because the Czech and Slovak economies are so intertwined (they are, in fact, a single economy), there would be enormous problems with the supply of raw materials and manufactured goods, with payrolls that are now federal, with separate currencies, excise duties, and so on. The problem of declining demand already affecting our industry would obviously get worse, which would mean that production would continue to decrease steeply, and unemployment would grow. I don't have to remind anyone that this would completely upset our economic reforms. Yet "freezing" the reforms would be the very worst thing that could happen to us; it would be like suspending surgery while the operation is still in progress. What this would mean to the "patient" is more than obvious.

Moreover, both republics would lose their defensive capability — a situation particularly grave where surrounding state borders are under dispute. From the point of view of security, separation would be a hazardous act.

The demise of Czechoslovakia would destabilize our entire region. Our geopolitical position has taught us that things that can be got away with in Southern Europe cannot necessarily be got away with in Central Europe. The instability this would lead to in our area, and on the whole continent, can scarcely be predicted, nor can it be predicted how our powerful neighbours, the former Soviet Union and the Federal Republic of Germany, would respond to a flashpoint next door. Our part in the integration of Europe, and in fact any assistance from the developed world, would be suspended for a long time to come.

Peaceful or not, the separation of our two nations would probably cool their mutual relations to the freezing point.

This too would have a detrimental effect on the lives of our citizens, who might well suffer an endless series of malicious political and economic sanctions imposed by their politicians. This would clearly make any subsequent attempts at close co-operation between the two countries, or any form of freer association between them, psychologically impossible — yet it is hard to imagine political or economic life in the new states without such co-operation. The unstable internal political situation, together with the economic decline and social unrest that the collapse of Czechoslovakia would bring about, would open the doors to a wide variety of undemocratic forces in both republics. Both Stalinists and Fascists would find common ground in demands to resolve the situation with an iron hand. We must face the possibility of a large exodus from both our countries, in the ensuing unrest. And we would almost certainly lose the international prestige and authority we gained after the fall of Communism. It would be a long, hard battle for two small countries in the throes of confusion to retrieve even a fragment of the renown they once enjoyed on the international scene as members of the Czechoslovak federation.

I have no wish to frighten anyone with apocalyptic visions and catastrophic scenarios. Were we to go our separate ways, I would do everything in my power to ensure that each partner suffered as little as possible. Still, I believe it is my responsibility to point out, in outline at least, that dividing up the country would not be an easy matter, and to explain why I do not wish this to happen. It would be a painful step with long-term tragic consequences for both republics, and both the Slovaks who periodically appeal to the Slovak National Council simply to go ahead and declare independence, and the Czechs who jovially cry in the pubs, "Let them go!" should disabuse themselves of any illusions they may have in this regard.

WHAT is a federation? What is a "federation that works"? Given the unrealistic constitutional visions we are presented with every day, these questions have to be answered.

Putting aside its internal differences, Czechoslovakia is unquestionably, in terms of international law, a single unified state. It has a single army with a unified command structure; a single common foreign policy; a single currency and a single monetary policy; common federal organs (Parliament, a government, a head of state); a federal legislative system (superior to the legislative system of its constituent parts); a unified system of taxation, customs and excise, and pensions; and, in fundamental matters, unified economic policies as well. Most federations have a single transportation, postal, and telecommunications network, and a basic energy supply system, though this is no longer essential, for the regulations may be unified and the administration of energy supply divided.

People who question even these minimum conditions aren't really in favour of federation, however frequently they may claim to be so.

The choice before us is clear: either we have a democratic federation, or we have two independent countries. There is no realistic third alternative, and anyone who offers such to his voters is misleading them.

It is impossible to be half a federal state and half not. Various such confederations and unions have existed for short periods of time, but they were always transitional. In our case, it is almost certain that the Czech republic would not accept an offer of confederation from Slovakia, for in the Czech political mind this kind of loose arrangement is strongly felt to be without much future. In Bohemia, such an idea would be understood — correctly, I think — as a pointless and expensive prolongation of the inevitable separation process.

WHILE, as I have said, I have a deep understanding of the historical, social, psychological, moral, and intellectual motivations behind Slovak national aspirations, I am far from sympathizing with how some (and I stress *some*) Slovak politicians exploit these aspirations, how they seek to reinforce them, how they draw on them and project them into their political practice.

Some very disturbing elements periodically occur and reoccur in Slovak politics. One example is a tendency to make quick, sometimes almost frightened and opportunistic changes in position. More than once I have observed work on the constitution made complicated by the fact that Slovak positions held yesterday are no longer held today, and no one can say whether positions held today will still be held tomorrow. And so proposals and demands that at first appeared marginal or absurd are suddenly taken seriously, and defended even by those who, until recently, rejected them — who now adopt them as their own. Unfortunately, they do so not out of conviction but for fear of appearing too half-hearted in their championing of Slovakia's interests.

Such changes in position have a single common direction: towards a "loosening" of the federation. Those who have demanded complete independence from the outset don't have to change much in their positions. But the rest — and they are still a majority — appear to be inching, subtly but systematically, towards the separatist position. Not many of these have openly abandoned the idea of a common Czech and Slovak state, but this, in fact, is what they are gradually doing. Hardly a day goes by that does not bring some new surprise position, one that looks "innocent" (that is to say, "federal") but is in essence very far from it. In an odd way these are confusing moves; I would almost call them "sidesteps". They not only betray a simultaneous fear of Slovak separatists and willingness to meet them halfway, but at the same time, in their ambiguity, betray a fear of the Czechs or of the Slovak federalists. (This, I must admit, offends me somewhat. No one need fear me; an unpleasant truth is a thousand times more pleasing than an attempt to humour me with equivocal formulations.)

And so it is not unusual for a sworn federalist to become, overnight, a proponent of confederation; for a hard-won and generous agreement on the division of powers, one that was declared the best possible arrangement, to suddenly be treated as "a bare minimum" or even the "cosmetic amendment" of a totalitarian federalism; or for someone, who knows very well what consequences it could have, to support the rapid adoption of the so-called pure constitution — that is, a purely Slovak constitution treating Slovakia as an independent state. (The argument that, after the acceptance of such a constitution, a portion of the powers would be delegated to the federation is an example of the ambiguity I was talking about. Clearly, once a constitution is passed, it is valid as passed, and from the day of its acceptance, not from the day it is formally to take effect — so in passing it a *de facto* state of dual legality will have been created.) And this is not to mention some of the particular ideas that have come up, such as the idea of a Slovak home guard. Everyone knows it means the prototype of an independent army, but no one says so out loud; instead the talk is of a "war on crime" — as if there were no police force to wage that.

What I consider the worst, however, is a kind of organized stirring-up of Slovak public opinion through half-truths and outright falsehoods. The less authority the central government has, the more it is accused of centralism (it could not behave centristically even if it wanted to, because it doesn't have the necessary instruments); the Federal Assembly is presented as the oppressor of the Slovak nation — despite the fact that a few nationalistic Slovak representatives in it can (and sometimes do) block any legislation they wish. Expressions of Fascism and anti-Semitism are condoned, and anyone who points this out is declared to have slandered Slovakia. Popular outrage is systematically directed against federal institutions as the alleged source of every kind of misery in life, while the good work they do for all citizens in both republics is passed over in silence. It is so easy and, at the same time, so irresponsible to garner applause by declaring in some public square that Slovakia has been robbed by the federation. If I were to call out in a Czech square that the federation is robbing the Czechs, I would no doubt be applauded as well. But those who say such things know very well that all federal revenues and expenditures are open to public scrutiny and were approved by the Federal Assembly. Why do they say them? Only to muddy the waters, only to gain popularity among the people and thus gamble with their fate.

What I have just written may displease some in Slovakia. But, as far as I am concerned, the Slovak nation is a mature nation like any other, and I refuse, in its own interest, to treat it like an immature child from whom certain things must be hidden, and whose easily wounded sensitivity requires delicate handling. Much harm is done to the Slovak nation by those who drive it into this childish position by constantly professing themselves offended on its behalf, and by constantly demanding the right to "special treatment" for the Slovak spirit.

This is playing with fire, and it's a game that provokes Czech politicians to do the same, thus further provoking the Slovaks. It is a vicious circle driven more by vanity and spite than by an interest in the truth. It no longer matters who started it; all those who indulge in it, without exception, are trifling with the lives of the citizens.

IF I'M not mistaken, it was I who some time ago first used the expression "authentic federation". I shouldn't be too eager to associate myself with it, since today this notion is not in very good odour. Among Czechs, it is connected with the prospect of a disintegrating federation and the retreat of Czech policies in the face of increasing Slovak demands. In Slovakia, on the other hand, it is perceived as a high-falutin expression for a new Czech centralism or unitarism.

When I used the expression in the past, I had in mind nothing more than a genuine federation — one that was democratic and just, an outgrowth of the free will of both nations and respectful of their autonomy. I opposed it to the federalized totalitarianism we had had before, which was purely formal — that is to say, inauthentic.

Of course, I still stand behind this idea of a federation. But I do not mean a federation that the republics think of as alien and hostile, as something that frustrates their aspirations, as a necessary (or perhaps pointless) evil, as something established over their heads merely to limit their sovereignty. Such a federation — a federation conceived as oppressor and policeman — would indeed make no sense whatever.

My understanding of an authentic, democratic federation is quite the opposite. It is the expression of a common will and a free decision; it is something created together, a common job to be done, a structure that exists to help the republics, to augment their sovereignty and their potential. It is a bond that exists because it is to the advantage of both sides.

The constant attempts to weaken everything federal and strengthen everything related to the republics (even in areas where it is clearly a disadvantage, or utterly impractical) derives from the *a priori* assumption that everything federal is bad, hostile, and restricting, and that it is therefore necessary to keep federal powers to a minimum. But if the republics understood the federation to be something that existed, or could exist, for their benefit, then they would have no reason to wish to weaken it, but rather would want to strengthen it, for in strengthening the federation, they would be strengthening themselves.

In short, I'm in favour of a federation which the republics create, in the fullest and best sense of the word — not one they see as something tertiary and alien, suspended over them as a bureaucratic entity without territory or population, and therefore one they resist. I'm convinced that in our case a co-operative federation is possible, and I am convinced that most citizens want a federation of that kind. The burden is primarily on those of us who have found ourselves at the centre of politics to plan such a federation, offer it to our citizens, then gradually build it as we have planned it. This is not just a legislative task. It is a great political task, and therefore a psychological and moral task as well. It demands foresight, and the courage to set the common interests of the citizens above the temptation to curry immediate favour by making federalism an enemy that can be blamed for all the misery in the world.

EARLY in 1991, at one of the first of our meetings on the new federal constitution, Slovak premier Ján Čarnogurský came up with the idea of a treaty that could be drawn up between the Czech and Slovak republics. None of the other Slovaks present supported it, and the Czechs were utterly shocked by the idea: a treaty between two states — that is, an international treaty — what else was it but a demonstration of the independence of both republics, and an attempt to establish their coexistence on the basis of a mere treaty, not on a federative basis?

This was followed by half a year of complex negotiations during which the idea of a treaty slowly gained the support of other Slovak political forces, and even ceased to shock the Czechs. It was as though the Czechs began to sympathize with the Slovak point of view and to understand the reasons leading the Slovak side to call for a treaty. Several times in the past, the coexistence of the Czechs and Slovaks was based on certain written or at least oral understandings between their political representatives. Those understandings were always broken, or not upheld, by the Czech side. The Czechs paid little attention to this; the agreements were forgotten and today only a handful of Czech historians are aware of them.

In Slovakia, on the other hand, this history of unkept agreements is still vividly remembered, and it was one source of the calls for a new treaty. This time, the Slovaks wanted an agreement that would be truly binding, one that would be a properly executed, legal act. At a constitutional conference in Kroměříž in June 1991, attended by leaders of the main political parties, the Czech side finally accepted, in principle, a modified version of such a treaty, involving an agreement between the Czech and Slovak national councils.

As an advocate of the federation, I don't think a common Czech and Slovak state can be based merely on a treaty between the two republics. Only a proper federal constitution can establish a genuine federation. Even so, I see no reason why a federal constitution could not be preceded by a treaty in which the representative bodies of both republics agreed on the foundations of a common state — that is, on the principles of a federal constitution. The Federal Assembly would then work out and ratify a constitution in the spirit of those principles, and the treaty would stand behind it as the source and origin of its legitimacy. Such a treaty, of course, could not be a treaty in the sense of international law; the republics as they are today lack the appropriate legal status for that. Nevertheless, what is not forbidden is permitted, and there is no law preventing the national councils from concluding with each other, in the name of their republics, an agreement on the constitutional form of a common Czech and Slovak state.

So far, no such agreement has been reached, but a new round of talks on the future of the state, its form, and its constitutional and political system will probably take place after the election. In any case, such an agreement or treaty — as a genuinely fundamental and free expression of the will of both republics — would be a clear confirmation and expression of the sovereignty of each republic: both partners, in concluding it, would be visibly demonstrating their autonomy and would thus satisfy the principle often emphasized (in Slovakia, at least) of a "grass-roots federation". In its own way it would be a stronger, more productive expression of the autonomy of the republics than a mere unilateral declaration of independence, which would not deal with what the consequences would be for the common state. The present existence of a federal state would not be called into question by such an agreement. On the contrary, the agreement would confirm the concept of democratic federalism I was talking about.

The principle of such an agreement — which is now, it would seem, generally accepted — does not cause me great worries.

The problems will lie elsewhere: in the specific terms of the agreement, in whether it manages to express generally agreed-upon ideas about the form the common state will take, what its internal structure will be, what powers will be delegated to it, and how they will be exercised. On these matters there are still many unresolved conflicts, and much remains to be elucidated.

But here, too, a referendum could help. If it turned out in favour of the federation, it would provide both national councils with a relatively clear directive and a clear commitment, and could be followed immediately by an agreement between them. This would open the way to the creation and enacting of both republican constitutions, as well as a federal constitution — or, more modestly, the main obstacles to such constitutions would at least be overcome.

THERE is a general consensus today that the present structure of our legislative assemblies, and the relations between them, are not good. That is why, in my proposal for a federal constitution, I have tried to simplify this structure on the federal level. I have tried to rationalize it and, at the same time, adapt it to my notion of a democratic federation as the common creation of the two republics that constitute it.

In my proposal, the Federal Assembly, as the Parliament of the common Czech and Slovak state, would be a unicameral body of two hundred representatives elected from all across Czechoslovakia. It would correspond roughly to the present Assembly of People, but the significant difference would be that the "minority veto" would relate to all its legislation. That is to say, even if there were more Czech than Slovak representatives — as there would be, given the larger Czech population — representatives from each republic would vote separately on every issue, and legislation would pass only if it was accepted by an absolute majority in each part of the Assembly. In other words, the voting procedure would be as it is today in the Assembly of Nations. This would be the first check against the representatives from the larger republic outvoting the representatives from the smaller.

I have also proposed a new body, to be called the Federal Council, standing completely outside the Federal Assembly. It would be a small body, with thirty members, and would therefore be more functional. Membership would be drawn from the republican parliaments in the following way: the chairmen of the Slovak and Czech parliaments would automatically be members, and would take turns chairing the Federal Council; there would also be fourteen members from each of the Czech and Slovak praesidia, delegated directly by the republican parliaments. If a praesidium had fewer than fourteen members, the rest would be made up by representatives from the plenum.

The Federal Council would have the right to return legislation to the Federal Assembly, which would then have to pass it with a larger majority. It would share in some basic federal decisions (declarations of war, states of emergency). It would appoint judges to the Federal Constitutional Court and, with the Federal Assembly, it would elect the president. It would have several other powers as well.

Setting up such a Federal Council would effectively eliminate the impractical two-track system that exists now, in which the republics are represented twice: once in their own republican assemblies, and once in the Assembly of Nations, the second chamber of the present Federal Assembly. In the republics, representatives to the Assembly of Nations are perceived as second-class representatives. My proposed Federal Council would eliminate this stigma, since in the Council members of the republican assemblies would also constitute a federal legislative body. This would emphasize republican participation in federal decision-making, and the idea of the federation as a linking together of the republics would thus be given immediate substance.

In standing, the Federal Council would be comparable to a senate or a federal advisory body. I imagine it as the highest "council of the wise", representing the republics in its task of overseeing the operation of the federation, and ensuring that the federation did not act against the will of the republics. Members of the Federal Council, who would also be members of the republican parliaments, would continue to have their base of operations where those parliaments are. The Federal Council would meet only occasionally, whenever it was felt necessary. My draft constitution specifies who may convoke the Council and how, the voting procedures within it, and so on. An important element in my proposal describes the constitutional relationship between the president and the Federal Council: the president may convoke it; he may ask it to take a position on legislation he has doubts about; he may take part in its meetings and have a vote; and if it is meeting on his initiative, he may act as its chairman. If the president — as head of the common federal state — is to play an integrating role in our constitutional system, then it is only logical that he be connected with this body — that he be one of the "council of the wise" intended to be a counterbalance to Parliament.

The Public Against Violence came out in favour of a senate that would elect a hundred representatives from each of the republics and have its seat in Bratislava. From the point of view of constitutional law, this would probably be a neater solution, but unfortunately it does not bridge that gap between the "more authentic" representation in the legislative assemblies of the republics, and their "less authentic" representation at the federal level. Otherwise, I'm in favour of locating this new body, in whatever form it might take, in Bratislava.

I published my proposed constitution at a time when most Czech and Slovak politicians were leaning towards the idea that the constitution did not require any prior agreement or treaty between the republics, when all that was felt necessary was a certain declaration of intent to coexist within a single state, from which the constitution would then derive. The proposal accordingly assumes such a declaration. Nevertheless, it seems to me that the idea of a Federal Council is extraordinarily in harmony with the idea of a prior agreement. If our federation, defined by its constitution, is derived from an agreement between the two republics, then the Federal Council, as an instrument of "republican control" over the federation, can be understood to have a duty to ensure that the principles of the original agreement are respected.

EVEN though the clause enshrining the leading role of the Communist Party in society has long since been struck down, our present constitution still in fact assumes that leading role. It still does not take into account the possibility of governmental or constitutional crises (either the minor ones common in all democracies, or the more serious, exceptional ones), because the underlying assumption is that the party will take care of everything. It doesn't take much imagination to picture a situation in which, under the present constitutional system, our country could be left without a government, a parliament, or a president. There is no provision for an emergency in which the president is unable to form a government that would enjoy the confidence of Parliament. In other words, there is no constitutional guarantee for the continuity of power, and there is even less provision for the operation of the state in an emergency.

In my proposal I tried, along with those who were working on it with me, to develop a system of constitutional measures to ensure that no unforeseen political, government, or constitutional crisis could occur for which there was not a proper constitutional response, so that there could be no danger of a *de facto* collapse of state power. We also tried to find the most appropriate system of checks and balances to protect the state from the abuse of power by any one of its organs or bodies. In our present unstable situation, I consider it especially important to find an optimal relationship between the legislative and executive branches of power, between the president and Parliament, the government and, of course, the Constitutional Court.

I will mention briefly one matter that aroused considerable interest: the position and powers of the president of the republic.

When I took office, I had the intense feeling that, in our country, the president was burdened with an inappropriate number of powers. I was astonished at what I could do. My conclusion was that when the Communist Party was in power it was of no consequence *what* the president's powers were, and that this was the only reason they were so broad. Over time, I came to understand that this feeling of mine was deceptive. It derived from the fact that in those first post-revolutionary weeks I had a great deal of influence and could not always distinguish clearly how much of that influence derived from my personal authority and how much from my powers as president. Moreover, that was a period of relative harmony, and it wasn't yet obvious how political conflict could paralyse the execution of state functions, including the presidential functions. It was only later, when I found myself face to face with the threat of political and constitutional crises, that I understood that the president doesn't really have much authority at all, especially to resolve such crises.

In all the post-totalitarian and post-Communist states, democracy is fragile, unstable, and untried. At the same time, these countries have to struggle with large problems that most stable western democracies are not at all familiar with: the revival of nationalism, the transition to a market economy, and the search for international standing as newly independent countries that are extricating themselves from their former satellite status. Simultaneously the threat of chaos in these countries is awakening the dangerous idea of "iron-handed rule". That naturally leads to an attempt to stabilize the emerging democratic institutions as quickly as possible, and to strengthen their authority, including the authority of the head of state. It is no accident that both Poland and Russia have decided on the direct election of the president by popular vote. This need not automatically mean that they will have some variation of a so-called presidential system, but it will certainly lead to a strengthening of the authority of the head of state.

I don't think Czechoslovakia should necessarily accept the principle of direct presidential elections. But I would be in favour of a certain strengthening of the president's powers. It would be enough to return to the position the president held in the First Republic, which derived from the constitution of 1920. This would make sense not only because the fragility of our emerging democracy requires safeguards, among which the powers of the president are paramount, but also because, if we are able to keep the federation together, the republics will certainly have (as they already have today, to some extent) greater powers than they had until recently. It will be all the more important, therefore, to balance those extra powers with something that encourages unity. The president could be one such binding element.

That is why, in my proposal for a new constitution, I suggested an increase — not large but definite — in the powers of the president. First of all, the president should probably not be recallable by Parliament. This power was not in the constitution of 1920, and it is not usual in other countries where the president is elected by Parliament. (In this case, the government is usually responsible to Parliament for the execution of the president's function — which is why some presidential decisions must also be signed by the relevant minister.) This principle is one of the guarantees of the stability and continuity of the power of the state. Where the government falls continually, or there is eventual dissolution of Parliament, someone must remain in place who will guarantee continuity and will not be dependent on other institutions.

Today the president must sign every piece of legislation passed by Parliament. In my proposal, while I didn't make it possible for the president to send legislation back to Parliament for further debate, I did enable him to turn to the Federal Council in cases of doubt, and initiate a re-examination of the legislation. If the Council then saw fit, it could return the legislation to Parliament.

Further, I proposed that the president not be compelled to recall individual ministers if Parliament expressed a lack of confidence in them; Parliament would have to express a clear lack of confidence in the entire government, at which point the president would have to dissolve it. This proposal had a different reason behind it: to strengthen the responsibility of the ministers to the government and the government to its ministers. A minister would know that, if he had a conflict with Parliament, it would threaten the existence of the entire government.

Finally, I proposed that if Parliament expressed non-confidence in three governments in a row, the president should be able to name a caretaker government, dissolve Parliament, and, until a new Parliament is elected, pass laws by decree (which laws would of course require subsequent parliamentary approval; the point is to avoid having to stop the legislative process for several months). This was a substitute for the present rather debatable provision for "legal measures" that can be passed by the praesidium of the Federal Assembly.

The president should also have certain enhanced powers, again limited by Parliament, in cases where the country's existence is in danger. This provision is especially important given the present unsettled situation in our region.

These proposals were based on my personal experience.

The powers I recommended were not excessive or unusual. The danger of abuse was small though still present, but this is always true. In any case, we must understand that the constitutional powers of leaders and institutions have to be thought through and balanced in such a way that they can, on the one hand, assure the smooth functioning of the state, and, on the other hand, make it impossible for any body to arrogate excessive power to itself, whether that body be the president, the government, or even Parliament. The remarks of the lawyers who prepared the 1920 constitution point expressly to this danger. They saw in the presidency a certain guarantee against a possible collective arbitrary rule by Parliament, just as Parliament is a guarantee against arbitrary rule by the president or the government.

THE POLITICAL parties occasionally accuse me of being against political parties. That of course is nonsense: the association of citizens in the widest possible variety of organizations, movements, clubs, and unions is an essential condition of every highly structured, civilized society. The freer and more cultured a society is, the more complex, varied, and rich is its network of different organizations. And, I dare say, the more difficult it is to get an accurate overview of that society. One of the most sophisticated kinds of association — and at the same an integral part of modern democracy and an expression of its plurality of opinion — is association in political parties. It would be difficult to imagine a democratic society working without them.

So — obviously — I am not against political parties; if I were, I would be against democracy itself. I am simply against the dictatorship of partisanship. To be more precise, I am against the excessive influence of parties in the system of political power. Where the political system — and thus the state itself — is too dominated by parties, or too dependent on them, the consequences are unfortunate. I have long thought this and now, in speaking with many politicians from democratic countries, my beliefs have been reaffirmed. They all warn me against an overemphasis on party politics, and urge us to be alert, so that we may avoid some of the terrible problems that can arise from it.

We have plenty of experience of our own in this regard. We need only read Ferdinand Peroutka's *The Building of a State* to understand that the dictatorship of party politics has been the bane of our political system from the very birth of Czechoslovakia. Even the number of ministers in our first independent government was determined not by practical need, but by the number of parties demanding a place in the government.

Excessive emphasis on political parties can have many unfortunate consequences. For example, loyalty to the party leadership or the party apparatus can count for more than the will of the electorate and the abilities of the politician. Party structures may even create a kind of shadow state within a state. A party's pre-electoral manoeuvrings become more important than the interests of society. Power-hungry people, under certain circumstances, can use their party membership, their servility to party leaders, their clever concealment behind the party flag, to gain a position and an influence that is out of all proportion to their qualities. Gradually the electors may come to be governed by people they did not specifically elect in the first place. All it takes is for a popular party, or a party with a popular program, to include such ambitious people on their party ballot, not because they would make good members of Parliament, but as a reward for their services to the party. Society will then live only from election to election, as all political decisions will be determined by the electoral tactics and strategies the parties adopt. The consequences of such behaviour in a society where all the ownership and property relations are being completely transformed, where a new legal and economic order is being created, and where the country is seeking a new international position for itself are difficult to imagine.

All one has to do is look around: a few months before the elections, electoral politics are already dominating political life. Half the news and commentary in the papers consists of speculations about which parties will ally themselves with which. There are articles about partisan bickering, bragging, and intrigue, predictions about who will join with whom and against whom, who will help (or harm) whose chances in the election, who might eventually shift support to whom, who is beholden to whom or falling out with whom. Politicians seem to be devoting more time to party politics than to their jobs. Not a single law is passed without a debate about how a particular stand might serve a party's popularity. Ideas, no matter how absurd, are touted purely to gain favour with the electorate. Parties formed for reasons of personal ambition compete for free air time. Coalitions are formed solely to create the illusion of size and weight. Normally, none of this would bother me; such ferment is, after all, part of democracy and gives it much of its character and colour. What troubles me is that, in our present serious situation, all this displaces a responsible interest in the prosperity and success of the broader community.

Is there a way of helping society to mature and form its natural political affinities, and at the same time prevent government by the people from being pushed out by government by party hacks?

Of the many possible ways of dealing with this situation, one seems particularly simple: through a decent electoral law. It is remarkable how little thought has been given to this option. The Federal Assembly did not even include it on its legislative agenda for 1991. Clearly the silent assumption was that we would retain the electoral law of 1990. In my opinion this would be wrong. One of the mistakes I made in my first term was not showing more persistence in the fight for a different electoral law. There were several of us struggling for it: Petr Pithart, Josef Vavroušek, and others. Everyone eventually dropped out of the fight, including myself, although I was among the last to do so.

To put it simply, the debate is between a proportional system, in which electors vote for parties which are then represented in Parliament in numbers proportional to their share of the total vote, and a majority system, where people vote for particular candidates and Parliament consists of those who win in the various electoral districts. My unqualified preference is for a majority system, but I would even be grateful for a system that combined elements of both.

In the 1990 elections, a slightly modified form of the proportional system prevailed. Each party had three lists of candidates in every electoral district: one for each of the two houses in the Federal Assembly, and one for the republican Parliament. Voters were presented with a sheaf of ballots from all the parties, and then placed three, belonging to the party of their choice, into the ballot box. The ballots were counted, and seats were allotted proportionally in the different assemblies. The electoral districts were large, some of them having well over thirty seats in Parliament. If a party won 20 per cent of the popular vote in such a district, the first seven candidates on its list would become members of Parliament for that district.

In this system, we could not choose specific candidates, and we certainly could not vote across party lines. The only thing we could do was circle, on the list of the party we voted for, the names of up to four people we preferred, thus increasing their chances of getting into Parliament. But inevitably, along with our first choices, we would also be voting for a lot of other people about whom we knew nothing. These people are in Parliament today, by our mandate, though we did not specifically choose them.

In the last election all this caused a great deal of mischief, but the consequences were not tragic. The political spectrum was not yet as wide as it is today, so voting for parties was easier.

But let us imagine how it might be in the next election. Imagine that in a given electoral district Václav Klaus is on one list, Jiří Dienstbier on another, Vladimír Dlouhý on a third, and Josef Lux on a fourth. We would still like to see all four of these gentlemen in Parliament, but we will have to make a hard choice because we can vote only for a single party.

The best system would be the following: the electoral districts should be much smaller, returning no more than two or three representatives. Electors would receive a single ballot and would vote for the candidates of their choice either by name or by party. The ballot would contain both party and independent candidates; voters could vote for up to ten candidates in order of preference, and the two (or three) with the most preferential votes would become members of Parliament for that district. I am not an expert in electoral law (which in any case is a rather arcane thing), but no one has been able to persuade me that such a system wouldn't work. I have come across only two objections.

The first is that it would be difficult or impossible for small but worthy parties to win any seats in Parliament. Thus various minority views or interests (such as an animal-rights party, for instance) would not be present at all in Parliament, which is not good: a democracy is recognized by, among other things, the degree to which it gives a voice to minorities.

This objection is the main argument against the majority electoral system, and I respect it. That is why I would admit the possibility of a combined system, such as exists in Germany. Two-thirds of the Parliament could be elected according to either the system I have suggested or another majority system, and the remaining third could be elected by proportional representation.

The second objection is that, if people were given an opportunity to vote for particular candidates, dangerous demagogues might get elected. Parties, so this argument goes, are a guarantee that this cannot happen, because they know their people and would not place anyone of dubious reputation on their list.

I reject this argument because it underestimates the voter. Is there any reason why the secretariat of a political party should be more reasonable than thousands of electors? Moreover, the argument is greatly exaggerated: it is unlikely that a questionable character could delude a whole electoral district. It might happen in one or two districts, but it couldn't become a general phenomenon. But more than that, aren't the chances of a party hoodwinking the voters greater than the chances of an individual doing so? Imagine a situation in which a popular personality forms a party with a memorable name and program, and easily — in a proportional system — gains a sufficient percentage of the votes. He may well be the only interesting person in the party, yet a whole group of nonentities could find themselves in Parliament without anyone knowing who they were, let alone voting for them.

It may surprise some that I have paid so much attention to just one law, out of the dozens our legislatures have passed or must pass, all of which are important. I have good reason for this: the quality of all our future laws depends on the make-up of Parliament — on the people in it and how they were elected.

IN THE meantime, Parliament has rejected most of my proposals and amendments, including my suggested electoral law and those designed to create a system of constitutional guarantees in the event of a constitutional crisis. These proposals were not accepted for a number of reasons. It must be said that, given our system of voting on constitutional matters in Parliament, relatively few votes are necessary to stop legislation. Some of my proposals were merely aimed at patching up the existing constitution, at averting the danger of a crisis. Unfortunately, the crisis I feared, and which my proposals were meant to forestall, did occur; our Parliament is now effectively blocked, and not only in constitutional matters. But in the long run, my proposals will be of no significance, for what is really at issue is the relationship between Parliament, the president, and the government, and their powers. These matters will have to be settled in the new constitution.

I intend to go on fighting for my long-range proposals, such as a new electoral law. I'm also convinced that my proposal for the establishment of a Federal Council is appropriate and will contribute to the creation of a genuinely democratic federation. These are things I am determined to fight for regardless of what position I hold in the future.

What I Believe

A LL MY adult life, I was branded by officials as "an exponent of the right" who wanted to bring capitalism back to our country. Today — at a ripe old age — I am suspected by some of being left-wing, if not of harbouring out-and-out socialist tendencies.

What, then, is my real position?

First and foremost, I have never espoused any ideology, dogma, or doctrine — left-wing, right-wing, or any other closed, ready-made system of presuppositions about the world. On the contrary, I have tried to think independently, using my own powers of reason, and I have always vigorously resisted attempts to pigeonhole me. I feel so open to everything interesting or persuasive that it is easy for me to absorb new ideas and fit them into my picture of the world.

I have not always been right. But my mistakes come from personal shortcomings — lack of insight, of attention, of education — rather than from ideological myopia or fanaticism.

I refuse to classify myself as left or right. I stand between these two political and ideological front-lines, independent of them. Some of my opinions may seem left-wing, no doubt, and some right-wing, and I can even imagine that a single opinion may seem left-wing to some and right-wing to others — and to tell you the truth, I couldn't care less. But most of all I am loath to describe myself as a man of the centre. It seems absurd to define oneself in topographical terms, the more so because the position of the imaginary centre is entirely dependent on the angle from which it is viewed.

Such an attitude is not popular these days. After decades of artificial uniformity, our society needs to learn how to think of itself in political terms once more, to restructure itself politically. This leads people to try to situate themselves "topographically". Every day the papers talk about how a particular politician or party thinks of itself as on the left or on the right, as left of centre or right of centre, as left of the right or right of the left or on the left centre of the right. But I really don't feel — even today — the need to position myself this way. To do so would *a priori* limit my freedom, bind me to something or someone, without revealing anything essential about my opinions.

I once said that I considered myself a socialist. I was not identifying with any specific economic theory or notion (and even less with the notion that everything should belong to the state, and be planned by the state); I merely wanted to suggest that my heart was, as they say, slightly left of centre. Rather than expressing any specific convictions, I was trying to describe a temperament, a nonconformist state of the spirit, an anti-establishment orientation, an aversion to philistines, and an interest in the wretched and humiliated.

It has been a long time since I referred to myself as a socialist, not because my heart is now in a different place, but because that word — especially in our linguistic context, where it has been so abused — is more confusing than precise. Though it is starting to mean something precise again today, it still does not offer what I would call a meaningful point of departure.

I avoid the word "capitalism" for a similar reason. I have never said or written that I am for capitalism or that I want to introduce it into our country. Like "socialism", "capitalism" is an ideological category popularized and vulgarized by Marxists, and I don't see why I should accept it from them — especially as the facile application of this category is broadly typical of a mentality that likes to simplify life by accepting similar ideological labels, and is connected with many dangerous phenomena of civilization that have no part in my program.

Though my heart may be left of centre, I have always known that the only economic system that works is a market economy, in which everything belongs to someone — which means that someone is responsible for everything. It is a system in which complete independence and plurality of economic entities exist within a legal framework, and its workings are guided chiefly by the laws of the marketplace. This is the only natural economy, the only kind that makes sense, the only one that can lead to prosperity, because it is the only one that reflects the nature of life itself. The essence of life is infinitely and mysteriously multiform, and therefore it cannot be contained or planned for, in its fullness and variability, by any central intelligence.

The attempt to unite all economic entities under the authority of a single monstrous owner, the state, and to subject all economic life to one central voice of reason that deems itself more clever than life itself, is an attempt against life itself. It is an extreme expression of the hubris of modern man, who thinks that he understands the world completely — that he is at the apex of creation and is therefore competent to run the whole world; who claims that his own brain is the highest form of organized matter, and has not noticed that there is a structure infinitely more complex, of which he himself is merely a tiny part: that is, nature, the universe, the order of Being.

Communist economics was born of an arrogant, utopian rationality that elevated itself above all else. When realized in practice, this utopian rationality began to liquidate everything that did not fit, that exceeded its plans or disrupted them. Censorship, the terror, and concentration camps are consequences of the same historical phenomenon that produced the collapsing centralized economy we inherited from Communism. In fact, they are two dimensions of the same error that began with this ideological illusion, this pseudo-scientific utopia, this loss of a sense of the enigma of life, and lack of humility before the mysterious order of Being, this turning away from moral imperatives "from above" and thus from human conscience.

YOU MAY sometimes hear it said that our revolution, and the forces that were then victorious in the election, defrauded the public because they made a secret of their intention to bring back capitalism.

It's true we didn't use the word "capitalism", and — as I've explained — I don't use it even now. But we have always stressed — not only during the revolution and before the election, but also (many of us, at least) long before — that we wanted a normal market system of economics. The program of breaking up the totalitarian system and renewing democracy would founder if it refused to destroy the basic pillar of that system, the source of its power and the cause of the material devastation it led to — that is, the centralized economy.

My conscience, therefore, is clean. I am as aware as the most right-wing of right-wingers that the only way to the economic salvation of this country, to its gradual recovery and, ultimately, to real economic development, is the fastest possible renewal of a market economy.

We have already set out on this path, and we refer to it (none too precisely) as "economic reform". The principles of the reform are set out in the government scenario approved by Parliament. The scenario, a step-by-step outline of this unprecedented task, is the outcome of long and comprehensive discussions among many economists, and is not just the product of Václav Klaus, the minister of finance, as many seem to think — although, thanks to his uncompromising stance, he had a most positive influence on its final form. There was general agreement on it, and on the need for it. It is the only meaningful alternative for this country.

For decades the population was bribed with money that, under normal economic circumstances, would have had to be invested in new technology, research and development, energy-saving schemes — in ways and means of increasing productivity and the quality and competitiveness of goods — but instead went to pay for our modest social security. We lived, as is frequently and properly pointed out, at the expense of the future.

Now the bill for all this is being presented to us, in the form of sacrifices. They are considerable, and greater ones await us. They are and will be as great as the loan we all took out of the bank account of our future. The size of this debt is directly proportional to the depth of silence with which we accepted the Communist exploitation of the future.

It is in our common interest that the reforms be fundamental and quick. The more half-measures we take, and the longer they drag on, the greater the sacrifices will be, the longer they will have to be made, and the more pointless sacrifices will have to be piled on top of those that are unavoidable.

We have to remember that we are only at the beginning. The cornerstone of the reform is privatization, and most of our companies and enterprises are still state-owned. Small-scale privatization — that is, the privatization of shops, pubs, restaurants, services, small businesses, and the like — is now more or less complete. Large-scale privatization — of the big state enterprises — is just beginning and will probably take several years.

I had thought the process would happen more quickly. For instance, I naively thought that by the time our first free election took place (in June 1990) the streets would be in full bloom with small private shops, pubs, and bistros. This one visible aspect of our country is only now beginning to change. I had no idea how great the problems connected with privatization would be, or how strong the resistance to it would be in the state enterprises, particularly in the mammoth state monopolies. Wholesalers, the food processing industries, and many manufacturing enterprises as well, are digging in their heels. Likewise, I failed to foresee how dramatically firms would be affected by the marketing crisis. (Of course, this is not entirely our own fault; the artificial marketplace built up over the decades in the Soviet bloc has collapsed.)

So I am certainly not in favour of "softening" or slowing down the reforms. On the contrary, I tend to worry about how slowly they are progressing.

THE ONLY thing that genuinely bothers me, because I think it is dangerous, is the way aspects of the reforms have become an ideology, and the way intolerant dogmatism, even sheer fanaticism, sometimes accompanies this process.

The market economy is as natural and matter-of-fact to me as the air. After all, it is a system of human economic activity that has been tried and found to work over centuries (centuries? millennia!). It is the system that best corresponds to human nature. But precisely because it is so down-to-earth, it is not, and cannot constitute, a world view, a philosophy, or an ideology. Even less does it contain the meaning of life. It seems both ridiculous and dangerous when, for so many people (and often, paradoxically, for those who over the years never uttered a single word of protest against the Communist management of the economy), the market economy suddenly becomes a cult, a collection of dogmas, uncompromisingly defended and more important, even, than what that economic system is intended to serve — that is, life itself.

Political parties and tendencies always have differed, and always will differ, chiefly in the relative importance they give to economic and social phenomena, in how they approach them and how they explain them, and in their opinions on the best way to organize economic life. There is absolutely nothing wrong with that. But that is as far as it goes.

Right-wing dogmatism, with its sour-faced intolerance and fanatical faith in general precepts, bothers me as much as left-wing prejudices, illusions, and utopias. Today, unfortunately, we often find that a straightforward analysis of specific problems and a calm, unbiased consideration of them are being pushed out of public debate by something that might be called "market madness". The cult of "systemically pure" market economics can be as dangerous as Marxist ideology, because it comes from the same mental position: that is, from the certainty that operating from theory is essentially smarter than operating from a knowledge of life, and that everything that goes against theoretical precepts, that cannot be made to conform to them, or that goes beyond them, is, by definition, worthy only to be rejected. As if a general precept were more reliable than the guidance we get, in dealing with the complexities of life, from knowledge, from judgement unprejudiced and unfettered by doctrines, from a sense of moderation, and, last but not least, from our understanding of individual human beings and the moral and social sensitivity that comes from such understanding.

A chemically pure theory is inapplicable and practically unrealizable. Life is — and probably always will be — more than just an illustration of what science knows about it. There is no such thing as a "pure system", anywhere. Social life is not a machine built to any set of plans known to us —

which is why new theories are constantly being fashioned: the flow of life, which is always taking us by surprise, is the only permanent challenge to the human spirit to strive for new achievements.

By the way, it is a great mistake to think that the market-place and morality are mutually exclusive. Precisely the opposite is true: the marketplace can work only if it has its own morality — a morality generally enshrined in laws, regulations, traditions, experiences, customs — in the rules of the game, to put it simply. No game can be played without rules. (It is no coincidence that many ancient religious books come with both a moral codex and something like a set of regulations for commerce.)

It is, of course, impossible to avoid projecting scientific knowledge into specific decisions, including decisions of the economic and political variety. Yet two things must always be kept in mind. In the first place, scientific knowledge can serve life, but life is certainly not here merely to confirm someone's scientific discoveries and thus serve science. And in the second place, science may be a remark-able product and instrument of the human spirit, but it is not in itself a guarantee of a humane outcome. A familiar example: science can lead people to discover atomic energy, but it cannot guarantee that they will not blow each other up.

Clearly, nothing can get along without the participation of powers as unscientific as healthy common sense and the human conscience.

Not even economic reform.

LET ME try to illustrate my thoughts with a story.

In 1990, I was present at a meeting of our three governments (Czech, Slovak, and federal) to decide on the basic outlines of a law on small-scale privatization. I supported the notion that employees in businesses that were to be auctioned off should be allowed certain advantages, in the form of either pre-emptive purchasing rights or loans at lower interest rates. My reasoning was based on a fear that the attractive businesses would be bought up by people who had come by their wealth in highly suspect ways (members of the former Communist *nomenklatura*, black-market currency dealers, and the like) and the less attractive would remain unsold, a burden to the state. I was anxious to have the small-scale privatization take place as quickly as possible, to avoid a strengthening of the economic (and thus political) power of thieves, and — because this would be the very first experience the public had with economic reform — to avoid it being seen as a social injustice comparable to the nationalization of businesses by the Communists forty years ago. If small-scale privatization resulted chiefly in enabling those with ill-gotten gains to use that money (essentially stolen) to start legal businesses, not only would it be immoral, it would be politically dangerous as well, because it could turn public opinion against the idea of reform.

Many arguments were brought forth in support of this, including the argument that at the outset of reform, in this completely transitional period when none of the market mechanisms was working yet, when the entire system of state ownership was being broken up in a revolutionary way, we could scarcely afford the luxury of a "pure market" solution. On the other side, many arguments were brought forward supporting a version of the law in which all interested parties would be equal, just as their money was equal, and no one would be given any advantages just for having worked in a particular business for a certain period of time. (I must say that one of the objections to our proposal was relatively convincing, and that later developments confirmed it to some extent:

many employees — managers, in particular — of shops and businesses in the grocery and restaurant sectors were, during the Communist period, skilled at enriching themselves at the expense of their customers, thanks partly to their mafia-like connections with people in the supply networks. It would be absurd, therefore, to give them any more advantages.)

The arguments on both sides were persuasive, but in fact this was a duel of educated guesses. Facts could not play a decisive role in our decisions because there were no data, not even approximate data. We did not know how great the interest in these businesses was, what kinds of people would take part in the auctions, how much money the interested parties had, or how much they intended to invest. And there were absolutely no informed prognoses about the possible course of small privatization, and its economic, social, and political consequences.

No one, therefore, could use facts to convince anyone else, and the result was that feelings were pitted against feelings, opinions against opinions, speculations against speculations. A vote was finally taken, and the position I supported was defeated by a small majority.

It is still too early to say whether this was for the best. I would of course prefer that it was. The auctions have been successful; there have been no major protests against the potential for injustice or immorality being built into the very foundations of our new economic system. Many businesses were indeed purchased by their employees. On the other hand, I often hear complaints that "all the power is being given back to the Communists". It is said that various brotherhoods and mafias of former high-ranking Communists are using front men to buy everything up. The auctions are allegedly creating a new "accumulation of capital" in the hands of the victors in the Communist *putsch* of 1948 and their followers.

I don't know that things are as bad as the gloom-sayers claim; personally, I doubt it.

But why have I mentioned this story at all? The proposal I supported at the time was obviously not, from the point of view of market economics, "systemically pure" (just as it is not "systemically pure" to prevent foreigners from taking part until the second round of auctioning). As a result it was criticized in the press, whereas the point of view that won out was praised for its systemic purity.

This was a typical situation. All the aspects of a possible solution and its complex consequences had to be weighed, though it was quite impossible to work the problem out simply by applying textbook precepts. Mere "systemic purity" is no guarantee of anything. The government has to accept, day in and day out, many "systemically impure" decisions that are correct, and perhaps the only possible decisions under the circumstances. Such is life! By the way, even large-scale privatization — our main bridge to a market economy — cannot be achieved without some elements that are systemically very impure, such as the principle of investment vouchers, by means of which state enterprises will be offered free of charge to the public, without regard for their market value. But if we are ever to see the real privatization of large enterprises, we have to employ such measures.

Whenever human instinct and unprejudiced considerations (if no statistics are available) tell us a pure solution is workable, it is obviously proper to choose it. But how are we to know when the solution will work — or when it isn't working any longer? How are we to know when a policy might prove suicidal, economically and politically? On what scales can we weigh and compare arguments based on economic theory with arguments based on practical economic policies? How are we best to collate all the points of view: scientific, political, social, and moral? In the end, it is always people who decide, backed by their personal responsibility, their personal thoughts, their personal assessments of the situation, their foresight. The less they are blinkered by ideology, with its tendency to transform theory into dogma, the better.

The mere ability to distinguish "systemic purity" from "systemic impurity" would enable one to do marvellously in examinations at university. In practical life, and in political decision-making, no one would get far without something more.

In short, I become deeply wary whenever I feel dogmatism or fanaticism breathing on me from any direction, even on the subject of market economics and its cherished "systemic purity".

Systems are there to serve people, not the other way around. This is what ideologies always forget. It is a fatal error. Communism has shown us, most graphically, where such forgetting leads.

ORTHODOX supporters of the market economy don't get their backs up only when they hear the word "state" or "social". They also bristle when they hear words like "conception", "industrial strategy", or "plan". The reasons for their indignation are understandable: those words create the suspicion that socialism, so diligently driven out, is surreptitiously creeping in through the back door, bringing with it the smug conviction that the state can, and ought to, organize production for industry, lives for people, and a future for society.

In our circumstances, when so many habits and stereotypes have survived from the era of Communist economics, and when so many powerful lobbyists are struggling, in various guises, to maintain the structures and practices that have made their lives comfortable over the years, vigilance is certainly necessary.

Even so, I think — and I am newly persuaded of this every day — that there are problems the marketplace cannot and will not solve by itself. In our country particularly — where the natural development of the market economy has been interrupted by force for decades, during which time many things have been stood on their heads, from energy production to the structure of industry to the organization of agriculture — we cannot depend on the influence of the fledgeling market mechanisms alone to solve everything for the government. Would that it were so; the government would have much less work to do. Unfortunately it isn't so, and to depend on such a simple solution could have fateful consequences.

ONE DOESN'T need to be an expert to understand that the marketplace alone cannot decide which direction Czechoslovakia should take in the matter of energy production. It is not just that, at this time, no one but the state can decide on the future of such monstrous products of Communist megalomania as the Gabčikovo Dam or the Temelín nuclear power facility. There is also the question of future energy sources. How can we ensure that the production of energy will not destroy our environment, that it will be efficient, that we will have a variety of decentralized energy sources that will not bind us economically and thus politically to anyone? Only the state can make such fundamental decisions.

We do not have our own oil. Where will we buy it, and how will we make sure that we don't become as dependent on those sources as we did in the past? Given our geography, enormous hydroelectric power dams are no longer a solution. How can we renew and expand the former network of small hydro plants, now destroyed? To what extent, and with what economic operations and instruments, shall we support such development? How shall we limit and eventually stop the mining of brown coal, which has helped to devastate almost all of northern Bohemia? With what shall we replace the electricity from the generating plants that burned this brown coal and polluted the air? How much should we depend on nuclear energy? It is clear that we cannot continue building gigantic reactors like that at Temelín. Should we begin building small, super-safe nuclear power plants? Or should we not be playing with nuclear power at all?

It is clear to me that we must have an energy strategy that looks decades ahead (as a matter of fact, the Ministry of the Economy has been working on this for some time now). Even countries with developed market economies, where everything evolved naturally and without violent interruption, have had to come up with energy policies appropriate to their own conditions. If France today gets 70 per cent of its energy from nuclear generating plants (with good safety records) and thus, it would seem, has essentially solved its energy problem, this is not simply the result of the natural operations of the marketplace (what could possibly be profitable about nuclear power in the short run?); it is a consequence, as well, of decisions it made after the Second World War.

Clearly the state will play a diminishing role in guiding the economy and deciding where, by whom, how, and how much energy should be produced, and to whom it will sell it at what price. Its role will be to come up with appropriate legislation and economic policies to encourage development in the desired direction, that direction being towards decentralization, plurality of sources, efficiency, ecological soundness, and diversification of foreign suppliers. So that the government can take the necessary legislative steps and make economic decisions that are co-ordinated and lead to the same goal, however, it must first know what it wants to achieve, and which roads lead in the right direction. It must, in short, have a strategy of its own, one that respects natural conditions, the structure of expected consumption, and many other things. It must have a goal and some notion of how best to get there. The legislation and the choice of economic instruments will then follow from the strategy. This approach guarantees that both the laws and the procedures are not merely outgrowths of economic theory, but that the theory has been applied to the specific conditions.

Our present industrial structure is an outgrowth of Communist industrial policies of the 1950s, when the main priority was heavy industry, and when many successful light industries and factories producing consumer goods were closed down. Everything was brought under central control, monopolized, and gradually made subservient to Soviet directives meant to serve the strategic needs of the Soviet Union, and later to directives from the Soviet-run Council for Mutual Economic Assistance — Comecon. In many sectors there was also an attempt to create a strange kind of self-sufficiency, under the slogan "The products may not be as good, but at least they're ours."

Now our industry will be undergoing a radical restructuring. Some branches will be trimmed back, others will grow; some enterprises will go bankrupt, others will be created; many will completely transform their production program; and the much-neglected tertiary sphere — the service industry — will grow as well. The result of all this will be great social movement, perhaps even upheavals, large shifting tides of labour, and unemployment. The chief authority in this situation will be the law of the marketplace, which is best able to determine what is viable and what is not. Nevertheless, if it is to happen quickly and without pointless catastrophes, this great restructuring will require the state to have its point of view too, and its priorities, drawn from a complex overview of the potential, needs, and position of our country. Of course, it will not impose these views by decree, but by projecting them into economic policies. In specific though indirect ways, the state must support firms that have a future, and make it hard on businesses that attempt to survive merely out of inertia, and to the detriment of society.

I believe that the large factories producing prefabricated concrete panels for high-rise apartment buildings will be replaced by a network of smaller brickworks. I have heard of a proposal (I can't tell yet if it is realistic) to co-ordinate the construction (or renewal) of brickworks with the phasing out of the brown coal mines, so that new job opportunities will be created for miners who are laid off. The feasibility of such a project would depend both on our energy plan and on the state of the construction industry. It could scarcely be expected to succeed on its own, through the sheer will of clever entrepreneurs. The state would have to support the plan, and help create positive economic conditions for it. But for that to happen, the state must know what it wants, have a strategy, and then act in that spirit.

Another example, very current now: the conversion of the armament industry. Obviously the state cannot invent new production programs for individual factories, nor can it come up with foreign partners to provide new technology and find markets for future products. Yet, having decided, for countless good reasons, to radically limit our production of heavy (offensive) military technology and stop its export, especially to unstable parts of the world and to countries supporting terrorism, we must — as a country — look for ways to encourage these enterprises, economically, to convert to other products.

Another thing: many foreign experts have warned us not to allow market forces to encourage wild and unregulated building sprees in our cities. Many western metropolises have paid dearly for this, and today bitterly regret not having carefully monitored their urban development. Such responsibility lies with the local administration — that is, the town and city councils — not the federal government. This is another area where the marketplace cannot be trusted blindly, but must be sensitively regulated. If the marketplace were given "systemically pure" freedom to do as it liked, one can imagine a ten-storey hotel suddenly appearing on the Isle of Kampa in Prague, or by the Danube in Bratislava, completely obscuring the view of their castles. For the time being, we are protected from such dangers by our inability to close deals with foreign investors quickly, by uncertainty about ownership and property rights, by confusion over competence to decide on such matters, and by our overgrown bureaucracy, which we have not yet managed to prune back. But what will happen when these obstacles are overcome? Now is the time to start thinking about it.

Because the Communists collectivized all the agricultural land, our government and parliaments have spent a lot of time devising and discussing legislation on the restitution of property rights, the privatization of state farms, and the transformation of agricultural co-operatives. But very little attention has been paid, in this transitional phase, to specific agricultural policies. Now this is coming back to haunt us: the farmers are up in arms and there are calls for a federal agrarian policy. Since we didn't have comprehensive policies worked out, the state has suddenly had to spend four billion crowns to purchase agricultural surpluses. This need not have happened had a well-thought-out government agricultural strategy already existed.

I could go on listing examples like this for some time.

WHAT am I trying to say in all this?

As far as the economy is concerned, the state, or rather the government, has three main tasks:

In the first place, it must quickly come up with legislation for the new economic system — legislation that will lay its foundations, determine the framework within which it will operate, and establish the "rules of the game".

In the second place, it must make some macroeconomic decisions concerning the economy as a whole, such as the setting of tax rates, budget outlays, credit guidelines, interest rates, exchange rates, and so on.

In the third place, it must establish specific "everyday" economic policies that will determine matters like the selection of firms to receive government business or to be given government support, interest credits, or loan guarantees; or when important foreign contracts should be signed, tax relief granted, and the like — in other words, when the government should react to day-to-day economic developments in the country.

In my opinion, the government cannot fulfil any of those three tasks properly — certainly not in our special historical situation — if it doesn't have a firm grasp of the needs and potential of this country, and a strategic and conceptual grasp of what the long-term aims have to be. Energy and agricultural policies, ideas about a better industrial structure, ecological aims, foreign policy — all of these must be carried out in a co-ordinated fashion. There must be something I would call a specific vision of an economically prosperous Czechoslovakia, something that goes beyond mere knowledge of the general laws of market economics and an interest in rapidly bringing them to life. I am convinced that everything the state (or government) does can derive only from such broad conceptual aims. Only against this background can all the proposed legislation, decrees, and micro- and macroeconomic decisions have a common logic, consistency, and meaningful inner architecture.

Unfortunately, I have to use the hated word "plan". It is

not enough simply to intend to build a market economy. We must know somewhat more about what we want to make of Czechoslovakia.

The importance of what I mean by a plan or strategy, by a concept or a specific vision, will, in future years, inevitably decline. The state should be less and less visible. It should gradually — as far as the economy is concerned — become a mere collector of taxes, taking from its tax revenues to pay for, or at least support, what cannot be expected to support itself right away but may pay for itself many times over in the future — like education, or research and development. Also, it should pay for things that will never pay for themselves but must exist if the state is to feel secure (the army), or for things that are simply part of the identity of a modern humane and cultural state, intended to serve people and society (a health service; old-age pensions; protection of the environment, the landscape, historical monuments, and culture).

In other words, once the train gets under way, it should be enough to check occasionally to see if it is going in the right direction. It should not be necessary to search out the direction continuously, to reinvent it in some ministry of economic strategy. The less the state is required to have a say in everyday economic affairs, the better.

Today, however, we are at a historical junction. We are choosing our future direction. And that requires genuinely comprehensive thinking. We must clearly understand where we are, what the locomotive we have at our disposal is like, and what dangers lie in wait for us on our chosen track.

Does such thinking make me a crypto-socialist? I think not, and I am confirmed in my opinion by conversations with different western statesmen who can by no means be accused of having socialist tendencies. More than once, they have expressed surprise that we seem to be surrendering too soon, as a state, our influence over the economic profile of the country.

I don't think this is so, but I do have the impression that we are always running to catch up, that we do too many things at five after twelve rather than at five to twelve, and that this is not just because of the complicated period we are going through and the complicated heritage we are coming to terms with. It is our own fault as well: we constantly let ourselves become distracted from our work by our petty warring, our tendency to wrangle among ourselves, our lack of mutual trust, lack of self-confidence (masked by political bravado), lack of generosity, by our fear of each other; in short, by our inability to bear the burden of our freshly won freedom.

To repeat: expertise that is not grounded in responsibility will hardly save us.

The Task of
Independence

THE OVERTHROW of the totalitarian system brought to an end the long era in which we were a satellite. It was astonishing how quickly and painlessly it happened. Confronted with the dramatic events in Central and Eastern Europe, and the stormy developments in their own country, the Soviet leadership evidently understood that it made no sense to attempt to preserve Soviet hegemony in this part of Europe. I don't know what Mikhail Gorbachev had in mind when he initiated *perestroika*, but towards the end of 1989 he obviously felt that it was impossible to stop the emancipation movements in the Soviet satellites. Even after our revolution, certain modified elements of superpower thinking still cropped up in the Soviet Union's policies towards us, right up until its disintegration. Many Soviet officials had not yet dropped their ideological prejudices and their bipolar view of the world as a world divided. Many of them, for instance, still saw the North Atlantic Treaty Organization as their potential antagonist, and it was hard for them to come to terms with the idea that NATO might expand to include their former satellites and thus move right next door. Nevertheless, I did not detect, either during our revolution or immediately after it, any direct or visible attempt to interfere in our political affairs, or even to refuse to recognize the legitimacy of the new democratic power.

Almost overnight, we became a politically independent country.

I don't mean that we liberated ourselves only because the Soviet leadership willed it, or that our freedom was handed to us as a gift, or was somehow prearranged. We had to take it and make it real ourselves, and we did. I only wish to say that we did not encounter any serious resistance.

The Soviets would undoubtedly have been happier to see Miloš Jakeš's conservative regime replaced by some kind of reform Communist leadership committed to *perestroika*. Nevertheless, when his regime began collapsing, they simply took note and did nothing to try to stop it. I even noticed signs of relief that our policies were in no way militant and anti-Soviet; on the contrary, we expressed the wish to maintain friendly relations with the Soviet Union, based on the principles of equal rights. (I still have vivid memories of my first long conversation with President Gorbachev. Initially, I think, he regarded me with a certain mistrust, as a somewhat exotic — and dissident — creature. Gradually, however, he warmed up and became communicative, recognizing, after all, that I'm a fairly normal person.)

Not everything went smoothly. For instance, the negotiations over the departure of the Soviet troops, which we set in motion immediately after the revolution, were not easy, and I consider it one of the great achievements of our foreign policy that there is not a single Soviet soldier on our soil today. Likewise, negotiations to liquidate the Warsaw Pact and Comecon were difficult. In Soviet politics, prestige traditionally played a large role, and when the Soviets finally understood that they could not save these organizations, they were concerned that their dismantling at least not be perceived as a defeat.

Some radicals have taken us to task for not quitting the Warsaw Pact immediately. For many reasons, we felt it wiser not to take this confrontational route. Doing so would have deprived us of any influence in the outcome of the organization. In any case, the forces of the Warsaw Pact had already invaded us once, and we could not be indifferent to it. We felt, therefore, that it would be better to take an active role — with other members — in working towards its early demise. Czechoslovakia worked hard to achieve this, and subsequent developments confirmed that our policy was the right one: the Warsaw Pact no longer exists. It was enormously satisfying to me when I presided over its final "self-destruction" in Prague.

And so, after many decades, Czechoslovakia has become independent again. It has become an autonomous entity on the international political scene and must now, independently, find a direction and a place of its own in this immensely complex terrain, with its thousands of interlocking interests of the most varied kinds. In other words, it must seek its own international political identity.

Independence is not just a state of being. It is a task. And fresh independence, such as ours, is a particularly complex task. We must fill it with substance and meaning, give it a specific form, and ensure that it will not merely be a new burden but that, on the contrary, it will bring benefit to all its citizens, who should experience independence as something worth fighting for, something worth defending, and something worth holding dear.

SEEKING the substance of our own independence today means, above all, seeking a new home for ourselves in Europe and in the world, seeking new relationships with those around us.

We have no wish to be anyone's satellite. Neither do we wish to float in a vacuum, thinking we can be sufficient unto ourselves, heedless of anyone else. Even less do we wish to become a buffer zone or no man's land between what was once the Soviet Union, enormous and explosive as it is, and democratic Western Europe.

Thanks to our geographical position, our fate is bound up far more closely in the wider events of Europe and the rest of the world than is the case in many other countries situated in less exposed positions.

To seek our new place on the political map of the world, we must — perhaps more than others — transcend the horizon of our own narrow interests and develop a broader idea of the way we wish the world to develop. Then, in that spirit, we must involve ourselves in those developments.

Our foreign policy has attempted from the outset to do this. It derives from four principles.

THE FIRST one is this: when the Iron Curtain collapsed, the basic obstacle to European unification collapsed as well. We must strongly support everything that contributes to such a unification. Today, for the first time in its history, this continent has a realistic chance to evolve into a single large society based on the principle of "unity in diversity". Evolution in that direction is not only in its essential interest (for political, economic, security, and broadly cultural reasons), but in the global interest as well. For decades, Europe has dragged the rest of the world into deadly conflicts. Today, there is hope that it can radiate — as a unifying entity — the spirit of peaceful co-operation.

THE SECOND principle is that this community must rely fully on the spiritual, intellectual, and political values that in recent decades have been maintained, cultivated, and practised in the democratic countries of Western Europe. I mean values like political and economic plurality, parliamentary democracy, respect for civil rights and freedoms, the decentralization of local administration and municipal government, and all that these things imply. I'm convinced that this is the only practicable alternative for Europe as a whole. It does not mean adaptation to something alien; it means, on the contrary, that nations once forcibly alienated from their own traditions, roots, and ideals are once again finding themselves; it means their return to a road they once travelled, or longed to travel, or were potentially destined to travel, as inhabitants of the same European spiritual and intellectual space. (This is how the popular slogan about our "return to Europe" should be understood.)

THE THIRD principle recognizes that Europe has deep ties with the North American continent, its younger brother. Three times in this century, North America has helped save Europe from bondage. Three times, it has helped freedom and democracy triumph in Europe. It cannot go on defending Europe for ever (and we hope it will no longer be necessary) but it is connected in such an essential way with Europe — by its culture, its values, and its interests — that the integration and emancipation of Europe should not be allowed to disrupt that natural affiliation. The peaceful alliance of these two parts of the world could, on the contrary, be one of the main stabilizing factors on a global scale.

FINALLY, the end of the Soviet Union's superpower hegemony does not mean that the nations that once constituted the Soviet Union should be cut off from Europe, or rather from the Euro-American world, and driven somewhere far beyond its borders. On the contrary, it means that their journey to democracy must be supported. It is in the interests of the whole world that these countries become democratic. The great rising of democratic forces that caused the

August *putsch* of 1991 to fail was clearly a milestone in this direction. Without in any way diminishing the historical importance of Gorbachev's *perestroika*, I would say that it was a curtain-raiser, and that the first act of the real drama is only now beginning — the drama of the genuine and thorough transformation of this empire into a community of free nations and democratic states. I surely need not emphasize how important it is to our future that this drama unfold well, quickly, and peacefully.

The momentous changes in the Soviet Union after the August *putsch*, which the *putsch* provoked and accelerated, were immensely important. It was clear that things eventually had to turn out the way they did, yet the process might have gone on much longer without the unsuccessful *putsch*. The Soviet empire was artificially glued together; the republics were moving in the direction of independence anyway; the whole country was ripe for a transition to real democracy, and *perestroika* was already exhausted. In that regard the collapse of the Soviet Union was a change for the better.

Naturally there are still hard times and many problems ahead as the individual republics seek to establish mutual relationships with each other and solve economic and military questions. But the general trend, it seems to me, is historically necessary and to the benefit of the whole world, of Europe, and of our country. Any potential danger from the east is immeasurably diminished to the point where I would say that there is now no threat of such a danger at all.

The threat of local conflicts, however, remains. So far, they are limited to Nagorno-Karabakh, but under certain circumstances a spark could spread the conflagration. One can imagine rivalry over the Crimea, and various local and civil conflicts, not just between republics, but within republics as well. There may still be some dramatic developments; nevertheless I think that, in its present phase, this community is no longer a threat to the world around it.

As for Gorbachev, though I had felt for some time that his policies were exhausted, that his inner limitations were preventing him from looking reality in the face, that instead of taking a certain course of action in time, he took it too late, and that he might have avoided some mistakes had he been more farsighted, I did not foresee how quickly and bloodlessly he would be stripped of his position. Gorbachev is, after all, an energetic, aggressive, determined, and flexible politician, quick to adapt to new situations. So the fact that he was swept so swiftly not only from political office but from the political scene was surprising, though it was a natural development. The era of *perestroika* and endless compromise, and of the whole reform Communist idea, had finally come to an end.

DIFFERENT opinion polls have shown that the public supports our present foreign policy. Indeed, given the limitations inherent in the present circumstances, we have accomplished a lot. We have renewed genuinely friendly relations with all the democratic states in Europe, and with many beyond Europe. With some countries, like the U.S.A., we have not enjoyed such good relations since our country was created in 1918. With others, we have never ever had such good relations. Relatively quickly, Czechoslovakia has become a respected independent country that enjoys widespread sympathy and trust, and in fact many rely on us to be a point of stability in an unsettled region. Our international initiatives have been welcomed and appreciated, and some ideas that were first articulated by Czechoslovak politicians, or by our diplomats, have caught on in the international scene.

From a long-term perspective, of course, these are only the first small steps. We will have the main task ahead of us. This is true of our "return to Europe".

One of the oldest centres of European political culture is the Council of Europe. Its goal is neither economic integration nor mutual security, and therefore it exists somewhat in the shadow of other European organizations. Nevertheless, it is a forum in which European standards in human rights and the rule of law have been developed and refined over the years, where democratic mechanisms are cultivated, where the principles of civil society are articulated, and where broad political dialogue is developed. So far, it is one of the few forums where most of the countries of Europe can confront their political problems together, give each other the benefit of their experience, look for different means of co-operation, and create common norms. Czechoslovakia was admitted as a member of the Council of Europe on February 21, 1991, but we have a long way to go before we can incorporate into our legal system everything approved of by the Council. We are still a long way from creating the political culture the Council of Europe has enshrined in its documents.

The entity that has gone farthest towards integrating Europe, and that is evolving the most dynamically, is the European Community. It is gradually becoming a *de facto* confederation of states, because its twelve member-nations have already delegated many of their powers to it. And they are preparing to hand over more: as we know, the European Community is getting ready for political and economic unity. Perhaps this is the beginning of a United States of Europe.

An associational agreement with the European Community was signed on December 16, 1991, in Brussels; it will be ratified in 1992 and should come into effect January 1, 1993. This is a great step forward that will have important long-term consequences for us, politically and, chiefly, economically. The agreement is "asymmetrical" — the process of exporting will be simplified for us, yet at the same time we will be allowed to protect certain domestic industries from competition from imported goods. It's the first step towards full membership, which we would like to achieve by the end of the decade. But we are still far from that point. Even some countries with developed market economies, like Sweden and Austria, still have a long way to go before becoming full members and it will be some time yet before we can hope to find a home, or rather an aspect of our home, in the European Community.

Of course, a lot will depend on the future policies adopted by this Community, and what form it takes. This is the subject of a good deal of talk now, because the European Community too is weighing the new situation in our continent, and considering how best to respond to it. It may well create a category like associate membership, which would enable other countries to advance more quickly to full membership.

The civil war in Yugoslavia has provided a test of co-operation in Europe. Together with Hungary and Poland, we have tried to co-ordinate our policies with that of the European Community. The issue is so complex and sensitive that it did not seem like a good idea to take action on our own. We felt it wouldn't be long before Slovenia and Croatia would have to be recognized diplomatically. We were prepared for this; we wanted to be in the first wave of countries to recognize them, if the European Community did not do it as a whole. When the European Community finally did so, we immediately recognized the two republics as well.

We had had good relations — for instance, with the Slovenian president, Milan Kucan — before the recognition of independent Slovenia. We had a variety of contacts;

we sent a delegation to Slovenia, and there was bilateral co-operation between us. Now we want to send troops to Yugoslavia in the context of the U.N. peacekeeping forces. But we did not wish to do anything in isolation, anything that had not already been co-ordinated with other countries.

We are members of the Hexagonal regional association, which includes Poland, Hungary, Austria, Yugoslavia, and Italy. In the future architecture of Europe, such regional groupings will undoubtedly have a significance of their own, because they will guarantee co-operation among countries that are immediate neighbours and have the same problems. (It would seem that another regional association, the Northern Council, is working well.) But the Hexagonal is still in its infancy, in the stage of preparing common projects. It is too early to say how it will work in practice, and there are skeptics who have doubts about its future. Since the break-up of Yugoslavia, the organization has become inactive.

Czechoslovakia once came forward with the idea of closer co-operation among the "troika", three neighbouring countries with a similar past and similar problems: Poland, Czechoslovakia, and Hungary. A number of reasons led us to this suggestion; historical experience was one of them. Hitler's expansion made it difficult for these three countries to establish mutual relationships after the Second World War. When we suggested closer co-operation, many felt it would not work, believing that these three fragile, inexperienced democracies, each absorbed in its own immediate problems, could scarcely agree on anything, let alone "co-ordinate" their return to Europe. But the skeptics were wrong; co-operation among the "troika" is beginning to make sense, and all three countries are beginning to understand — just like the great Moravian emperor-prince Svatopluk, whose ninth-century kingdom included present-day Hungary, Slovakia, Bohemia, and western Poland — that they can achieve more in certain areas by co-operating than by working in isolation. But here too we are only at the beginning; we have a long way to go before we become another Benelux.

In June 1991, at President François Mitterrand's initiative, a conference was held in Prague on European confederation. This is another idea in the right direction — that is, towards the integration of Europe — but so far it is really nothing more than an idea, something to think about. It is hard to say what will come of it.

To summarize: wherever I look, I can see that we are only at the beginning of a long and arduous journey. But I don't feel despair. In the short time I've been active in practical politics, I've come to understand that politicians must never be impatient, and that they can never in good conscience say that anything is settled once and for all. Politics is one long, endless process. At first — influenced by the wild rhythm of our revolution — I wanted to have everything done at once, and would be infuriated when it proved impossible. Yes, certain things might have happened sooner, and I wasted some opportunities by not being forceful enough. But on the whole I have recognized that political time is different from everyday time. Nothing can be assessed in politics immediately; everything unfolds at its own speed. Similarly, the first small steps we have taken on the road to our "home" can be properly assessed only after some time has passed.

FOR WELL over three decades, our "home" in matters of security was the Warsaw Pact. It was more like a prison cell, but it was a home nevertheless, as even a prison cell can, in a sense, be home. As a state, we didn't have to worry about our security; others looked after it, in their own fashion, and all we had to do was obey orders. We have now divested ourselves of that "home", and must tend to our security ourselves.

The first idea that always comes up is joining NATO. I hear this advice all the time, especially from members of Parliament. It is not as easy as people seem to think. NATO is not a club of stamp collectors or pigeon fanciers, where you simply send in your application and they accept you as a member. In fact, you don't apply for membership in NATO at all; NATO has to invite you to join. And at the moment they are not about to invite anyone else to join, let alone former members of the Warsaw Pact. They have their own excellent reasons for this; one of them is that they know only too well how the alliance is still viewed by many former Soviet officials, and what reactions it might cause if NATO started moving closer to the former Soviet borders. From a purely military and strategic point of view, there is logic in the Soviet thinking: no country likes to see itself surrounded by a powerful alliance to which it has no access.

But even if we could join, our membership in NATO would be more symbolic than anything else, enabling NATO troops to operate on Czech and Slovak territory in time of war. It would not be true membership. For that, we would have to have a compatible communications and command system, and the proper weaponry, military toys that will cost billions and take years to acquire. But that is not the only thing. Membership in NATO assumes compatibility in other things as well, from economics to a more or less stable political system. As far as NATO is concerned, the most we can do at this point is begin co-operating with them, and then gradually, step by step, deepen our relationship. That we are of course doing, and will continue to do.

NATO too is reconsidering its future in the light of the new situation in Europe. It has already passed resolutions which make it clear that it is changing its military doctrine, and in fact its whole philosophy. This is understandable: Europe is no longer divided into opposing blocs; the west is no longer immediately threatened by the east. So far, though, there are no compelling reasons to dissolve the alliance. In the first place, the former Soviet military potential is still enormous, and no one can yet guarantee that, in that unsettled area, there will not be some reversal — though this is much less probable since the collapse of the August 1991 *putsch*. In the second place, the Soviet Union was far from being the only potential enemy. It is not hard to imagine other dangers, from within the former Soviet Union or from elsewhere. I'm not at all surprised that neither the Americans nor the Europeans are rushing to dismantle NATO. And the argument that NATO loses its meaning if the Warsaw Pact no longer exists does not hold up at all. NATO is truly a defensive organization, and truly democratic: members can withdraw at any time, and they have equal rights within it. Realistically, the Americans have and will always have a greater say in NATO than, say, Portugal; still, nothing would happen to Portugal were it to decide to quit NATO or eliminate NATO bases on its territory.

Nevertheless, I think that if the former Soviet Union poses no threat, and if the integrational processes in Europe proceed well, NATO will eventually change. It is not impossible — and I've talked about this more than once — that it may one day evolve, or be transformed, into a new pan-European security structure. I don't know how much longer American forces will have to remain in Europe (their number has recently been radically reduced), but the war in the Persian Gulf demonstrated that their presence in Europe can still be important. Whether they remain or not, one thing seems clear: the United States and Canada should always maintain security ties with Europe.

So far the only regional institution that includes all the

countries of Europe, the whole territory of the former Soviet Union, and the U.S.A. and Canada is the Conference on Security and Co-operation in Europe, originally founded in Helsinki in 1975 with the signing, by all the countries in Europe, and Canada and the U.S.A., of the Helsinki Accords. In matters of security, we have backed this institution from the beginning (as a reward for our many initiatives in this forum, Prague is now the permanent seat of the CSCE's secretariat). The CSCE has a bright future, and has the potential of one day becoming a genuine guarantor — in fact, the chief guarantor — of collective European security. It may even be the entity NATO will "serve", or into which it will eventually grow. More and more countries and politicians are grasping the future possibilities of the Helsinki process, some of whom were, until recently, very skeptical about it.

The CSCE will also intensify and deepen its work; it is becoming a more permanent institution, and is creating new mechanisms. In January 1992, the ministers of foreign affairs of all member countries met in Prague. Various resolutions were passed that were intended to strengthen the Helsinki system. Republics from the former Soviet Union have also been accepted as new members, and they are all eager to work within this association, because they feel it gives them a new chance. In July the important Helsinki II meeting will take place. It could become a milestone of sorts. Essentially the issue is that, until now, the CSCE could pass only documents recommending certain courses of action to its member governments, or documents in which those governments issued certain declarations. In the future, such resolutions could be binding; their implementation would be monitored, and failure to comply could bring sanctions. It would mean the creation of a new generation of Helsinki agreements which would, *de facto*, transform this institution into a loose alliance, and could form the basis of a genuine collective security system. As a matter of fact, there is already talk of setting up a "Helsinki" peace force — a proposal made in response to the civil war in Yugoslavia. In November 1990, I was at a CSCE summit in Paris where the Paris Charter was signed. This is an excellent and important document that allows for, or at least anticipates, such developments in the Helsinki process.

The Helsinki process, then, is another "iron in the fire", one that touches far more than just security matters. It is another way of achieving genuine pan-European political integration. Who knows — perhaps the Helsinki process may one day become a contractual framework for some emerging European confederation. If I unleash my fantasy, I can easily imagine a confederating Europe whose guarantor or mediator is the Helsinki process, with a transformed NATO in charge of security, the Council of Europe as its political centre, and a gradually expanding European Community the driving force behind it. When something like that exists, we will be able to say with a clear conscience that we have found our European home.

But for the time being, all that is far away. It requires time, diligent work, endurance, patience, negotiating skills, and — of course — goodwill on all sides.

IT WOULD seem that the world, and Europe in particular, is moving away from the principle of bilateral agreements and towards the principle of multilateral agreements, alliances, and formations of all kinds. This is happening not only in the sphere of security, but in all areas of co-operation. It is a logical development, and a good one, appropriate to the times we live in, when almost everything is becoming global, when everything relates to everything else and fewer important things can be settled in isolation.

Nevertheless, for those of us who are building a new international status from scratch — or, as we say in Czech, in a green meadow — there are some bilateral agreements that are extremely important. They form a network that could be developed relatively quickly and could provide us with something to hang on to, the first signals of certainty, our first reason to feel that our new home is being built. In themselves such agreements are not the ultimate end of all our efforts (especially since, in our recent history, we have not had the best experience with bilateral agreements), but they can form a basis on which we can build.

Each of these agreements contains, or should contain, some form of security arrangement; each should include the possibility of immediate consultation in the case of threat, and should allow for mutual assistance or support. They should all conform to present European standards and should be as far as possible consistent with other such agreements; they should be based on international documents to which both parties are signatories, and take into account, or signal, the future integration of Europe. They should include a promise of support for our entry into international communities.

We signed a treaty with Italy on July 1, 1991. The most important aspect of it, particularly given our bilateral treaty with Germany, is a declaration that the Munich Agreement of 1938 — ceding Sudetenland to Germany — was null and void from the beginning.

A treaty with France, signed on October 1, also contains a "Munich" paragraph.

We signed a treaty with Poland on October 8, 1991, and a treaty with Hungary has been prepared as well. Included in them are security clauses providing for assistance in the event that one of the partners is attacked.

A treaty with Germany was signed on February 27, 1992. This is a particularly important agreement: our mutual relations will at last be fully "normalized" as between two democratic countries, prefiguring our life together in the united Europe of the future. Despite the speculations on both sides, everyone in Czechoslovakia who was worried that the property left behind by the Germans who were expelled from Czechoslovakia after the Second World War would be subject to restitution can now relax: there is no such clause in the agreement. We did, of course, make a conciliatory offer to the Sudeten Germans: it was in our own interests to admit that the expulsion of the Germans, and especially the way it was carried out, was in every way an inappropriate response to the crimes of the Nazis and the Henleinians. Of course, such an admission is not to the detriment of our citizens, who cannot be held responsible for the decisions and actions of their predecessors. The point is that wrongs must never again be redressed by new wrongs.

The final bilateral agreement was with the Soviet Union. The preparations dragged on because of disagreements over the security clause. The Soviet side suggested that each party to the agreement undertake not to enter into any alliance directed against the other. We could not accept such a clause because it would have been in conflict with the Helsinki Accords, it would have limited our sovereignty, and it would have prevented us from entering into any other alliance for the next ten or fifteen years, since the Soviet Union could have, if it wished, declared any such alliance to be hostile to it. Of course, we had no wish to enter any alliance aimed against the Soviet Union, but at the same time we didn't want to have our hands tied by such an uncertain formulation. (Who would arbitrate any eventual dispute?) We cannot know what future European security structures will emerge. There may be several different interim stages, and we have no way of knowing in advance what possibilities will be open to us. Furthermore, the newly integrating political and economic groupings in Europe have a security dimension to them as well, so that we could also be limited with regard to entering those. The Soviets wanted the same commitment from Poland, Hungary, and Bulgaria, but all these countries have rejected them too. Only Romania agreed to the security clause.

Since then, of course, the Soviet Union has ceased to exist, and the treaty, which was initialled but never signed, was eventually renegotiated with Russia and initialled in Moscow on February 19, 1992. It too included the "Munich" paragraph.

These six bilateral agreements are modern and democratic, recognizing the equality of both partners. They are not simply formal, but genuinely valid and binding, and advantageous to both sides. This is another small step towards our new European home.

ALL THESE things — the treaties, the international initiatives, the specific steps we have taken in foreign policy and diplomacy — must naturally have unifying aims.

I have already spoken of the aims of our foreign policy. But if they are to have a common *raison d'être* and meaning, and if they are to be logically related to each other, these aims must assume something more, something I would call the spirit of foreign policy. Just as a country must have its own spirit, its own idea, its own spiritual identity, so its foreign policy must have these as well.

Everything else must grow out of this essential spirit. It is what determines the face, or the style, of the foreign policy. This spirit alone can ultimately give our independence the specific substance, meaning, and profile it needs.

So what is, and what ought to be, the spirit of our foreign policy?

Its basic outlines originated and were shaped in the opposition movement of the last twenty years, in our emphasis on human rights and our nonviolent struggle to have those rights respected.

Yes, our policies — foreign and domestic — must never be based on an ideology; they must grow out of ideas, above all out of the idea of human rights as understood by modern humanity.

Freedom of the individual, equality, the universality of civil rights (including the right to private ownership), the rule of law, a democratic political system, local self-government, the separation of legislative, executive, and judiciary powers, the revival of civil society — all of these flow from the idea of human rights, and all of them are the fulfilment of that idea.

Human rights are universal and indivisible. Human freedom is also indivisible: if it is denied to anyone in the world, it is therefore denied, indirectly, to all people. This is why we cannot remain silent in the face of evil or violence; silence merely encourages them. Czechoslovakia has had bitter experience with the politics of giving in to evil; in its time, that policy led to the loss of our existence as a country. It is no accident, therefore, that we are especially sensitive to the indivisibility of freedom. We sent our units to the Persian Gulf to declare once more our support for that principle — not because we wanted to ingratiate ourselves with the Americans.

Respect for the universality of human and civil rights, their inalienability and indivisibility, is of course possible only when one understands — at least in the philosophical sense — that one is "responsible for the whole world" and that one must behave the way everyone ought to behave, even though not everyone does.

This sense of responsibility grows out of the experience of certain moral imperatives that compel one to transcend the horizon of one's own personal interests and be prepared at any time to defend the common good, and even to suffer for it. Just as our "dissidence" was anchored in this moral ground, so the spirit of our foreign policy should grow and, more important, continue to grow from it.

It should not, in other words, be a selfish, inconsiderate, mindlessly pragmatic foreign policy, to promote the interests of our own country unscrupulously, to the detriment of everyone else. It should rather be a policy that sees our own interests as an essential part of the common interest, one that encourages us at all times to become involved, even when there is no immediate benefit to be had from it. It should be, therefore, a policy guided by a "higher responsibility" in which the world and the global dangers that threaten it are seen comprehensively; a humane, educated, sensitive, and decent policy.

This higher responsibility is by no means a megalomaniacal feeling that we Czechs and Slovaks are better than all the rest, that we can show others what they should be doing, and that we know all the answers. On the contrary, among the traits of a policy so conceived are modesty and good taste — which, by the way, are qualities that always accompany genuine responsibility. Tact, a sense of moderation, of reality, an understanding of others, and an ability to make realistic assessments — these qualities are not excluded from this spirit, but flow directly from it.

Clearly, a dissident intellectual who philosophizes in his study about the fate and future of the world has different opportunities, a different position, a different kind of freedom, than a politician who moves among the complicated social realities of a particular time and place, constantly coming up against the intractable and contradictory interests that inhabit that time and space. But a person who is sure of the values he believes in and struggles for, and who knows he simply cannot betray them, is usually able to recognize the degree of compromise permissible in the practical application of his ideals, and to know when a risk becomes more than he can take upon himself.

Often it is possible to be one or two steps ahead of everyone else. For example, when I invited the Tibetan Dalai Lama here and was the first head of state to meet with him, many more pragmatic politicians warned me that China would be upset. As it turned out, China did not invade us in retaliation, nor did they cancel any contracts. But the Dalai Lama was subsequently received by many other heads of state. There was, of course, a certain risk in what I did, but I felt that, in the interest of a generally good thing, this risk could properly be undertaken. Similarly, pragmatists claimed that it was not tactical to establish relations with Boris Yeltsin. His trip to Czechoslovakia in May 1991 was his first official visit outside the U.S.S.R. as chairman of the Supreme Soviet, and the world still looked askance at him. In this case, too, decency paid off in the end.

On the other hand, it is not usually a good idea to be too far ahead of the pack. True, it's an easy way to glory, but the risk can far outweigh the actual significance of the good intentions. Moreover, one can easily lose touch with the group, and thus lose the chance of positively influencing it as well.

The sensitivity to judge whether we are about to make that inspiring step forward, or are, through a display of bravado, toying with fate and thus arousing only resistance in our partners, is not the sole property of cool, calculating pragmatists. On the contrary, they tend to lack this quality. It is just one more expression of the morally grounded responsibility I am talking about.

In other words: acting sensitively in a situation does not exclude morality, but is more likely to accompany it, be bound to it, and even derive from it, because it comes from the same source — responsible thinking, attentiveness, and a dialogue with one's own conscience.

SOMETIMES people say that, in my handling of foreign affairs, I am too much of an idealist, a dreamer, a philosopher, a poet, a utopian. I have no wish to deny anyone his impressions or his feelings. I merely point out that, if Czechoslovakia enjoys the respect it does in the world today, then it is due — among other things — to the kind of basic decency and humanity with which Communism was overthrown here, and the moral direction of our foreign policy.

Will this respect last, or will we soon lose it as a result of our incapacity to settle our domestic affairs in a reasonable way?

Beyond the Shock
of Freedom

I OFTEN think about what our country will be like in ten, fifteen, or twenty years, and I regret that I cannot, for a moment at least, leap over the hard years that lie ahead and look into our future.

That life is unfathomable is part of its dramatic beauty and its charm. So is the fact that we know nothing about our own future, except that some day we will die. Nevertheless, let me attempt to describe, briefly, the kind of Czechoslovakia I would like to see and strive for with my limited powers.

I will, in short, dream for a while.

IN THE first place, I hope, the atmosphere of our lives will change. The shock of freedom, expressed through frustration, paralysis, and spite, will have gradually dissipated from society. Citizens will be more confident and proud, and will share a feeling of co-responsibility for public affairs. They will believe that it makes sense to live in this country.

Political life will have become more harmonious. We will have two large parties with their own traditions, their own intellectual potential, clear programs, and their own grass-roots support. They will be led by a new generation of young, well-educated politicians whose outlook has not been distorted by the era of totalitarianism. And of course there will be several smaller parties as well.

Our constitutional and political system will have been

created and tested. It will have a set of established, gentlemanly, unbendable rules. The legislative bodies will work calmly, with deliberation and objectivity. The executive branch of government and the civil service will be inconspicuous and efficient. The judiciary will be independent and will enjoy popular trust, and there will be an ample supply of new judges. We will have a small (40,000 strong?), highly professional army with modern equipment, part of which will come under an integrated European command. A smaller, elite unit will be part of the European peacekeeping force. A well-functioning, courteous police force will also enjoy the respect of the population, and thanks to it — though not only to it — there will no longer be anything like the high crime rate there is now.

At the head of the state will be a grey-haired professor with the charm of a Richard von Weizsäcker.

We will, in short, be a stable Central European democracy that has found its identity and learned to live with itself.

CZECHOSLOVAKIA will be a highly decentralized state with confident local governments. People's primary interest will be in local elections rather than the parliamentary ones. Each town and city will have its own individual face and its own inimitable spiritual climate — the pride of the local authorities. Municipalities will finance their affairs from municipal taxes, rather than from transfer payments, and will no longer need to complain constantly about never having enough funds, or to seek revenue from the ownership of various enterprises. The governments and administrations of the different historical regions will be intricately structured: Moravia and Silesia will once again have their own regional governments, including their own assemblies; other regions (northern Bohemia? eastern Slovakia?) will have some degree of autonomy, though to a lesser extent.

The whole country will be crisscrossed by a network of local, regional, and state-wide clubs, organizations, and associations with a wide variety of aims and purposes. This network will be so complex that it will be difficult to map thoroughly. Through it, the rich, nuanced, and colourful life of a civilized European society will emerge and develop.

Life in the towns and villages will have overcome the legacy of greyness, uniformity, anonymity, and ugliness inherited from the totalitarian era. It will have a genuinely human dimension. Every main street will have at least two bakeries, two sweet-shops, two pubs, and many other small shops, all privately owned and independent. Thus the streets and neighbourhoods will regain their unique face and atmosphere. Small communities will naturally begin to form again, communities centred on the street, the apartment block, or the neighbourhood. People will once more begin to experience the phenomenon of home. It will no longer be possible, as it has been, for people not to know what town they find themselves in because everything looks the same.

Prefabricated high-rise apartment blocks and other kinds of gigantic public housing developments will no longer be built. Instead, there will be developments of family houses, villas, townhouses, and even low-rise apartment buildings. They will be better constructed, more varied, and on a more human scale.

Both the historical cores of our cities and towns, and their pre-war suburbs, will be sensitively revitalized and renovated in such a way that the specific charm of each is preserved while the risk of the buildings collapsing on people's heads is eliminated. It will no longer take a young married couple a decade of hard work, involving all their relatives, to find themselves an apartment. Once a varied network of competing construction firms and societies is created, many people will be astonished at how quickly a great deal can be done.

Existing high-rise housing estates, where so many people have made their homes over the last four decades, will be enlivened in different ways — some redesigned and altered, others gradually phased out to make room for something more adequate for the twenty-first century. People can — as we know — get used to anything, so why should they not get used to shops in apartment buildings, children playing in parks, and streets and squares that are more than just blank spaces on a plan?

The houses, gardens, and sidewalks will be clean, tidy, and well cared for, because they will belong to someone; for every piece of real estate, there will be someone with a reason to look after it. All the dead spaces, which in Prague, I understand, account for more than one-third of the city's land area — spaces that no one knows the real purpose of (are they meadows, parking lots, construction sites, rubbish dumps, factory yards, or a combination of all of the above?) — will be turned into something specific. Some areas will be intelligently built on, and others will be converted to parks or something else. Apart from completing the construction of the superhighways that form our share of the European network, we will have good local highways lined with trees, the occasional motel or rest stop, and gas stations owned by competing firms. Towns will not grow every which way, like tumours, without regard for the most efficient use of available space (and thus without regard too for the land and the countryside). Best use will be made of every square metre, since it will once again have a value and an owner.

In short, the villages and towns will once again begin to have their own distinctive appearance, culture, style, cleanliness, and beauty. We can't expect to become a Switzerland or a Holland; we will remain ourselves, but our outer face will stand comparison with these countries. We will not have to feel ashamed — either before ourselves or before foreigners — of the environment in which we live. On the contrary, that environment will become a source of quiet, everyday pleasure for us all.

THE RAILWAYS, transportation, communications, and distribution networks will probably be partly state-owned, partly private but under state control, and partly owned by companies in which the state has a stake. I truly don't know what combination will be best in our case; different developed countries do it differently. But I hope that natural development and wise decisions will create the optimum model.

Apart from that, everything will be privatized, including the largest enterprises. Business corporations will be the rule, but there will also be co-operatives, individual private owners, and other types of ownership. Foreign companies, firms, and entrepreneurs will obviously play a large role. Our economy can hardly be expected to recover without extensive foreign investment and a flow of capital in our direction. Firms of different provenance will be present, so we will not be excessively dependent on any single country. Large-scale privatization has been organized to ensure a respectable degree of participation by domestic investors. There is a great wealth of skill and enterprising spirit in our society. Were this potential to be continually pushed out of the way by foreign skills and entrepreneurialism, it might well lead to considerable social tensions, and it would not even be just.

As we know, money is the life-blood of economics. The circulation of money should be streamlined by a well-developed network of banks and savings institutions. Perhaps the single European currency now under discussion will be introduced here, but, if not, by that time our crown will be firm and fully convertible. A new and comprehensible tax system will have to be operating, including tax offices, tax advisers, and tax-fraud investigators — in short, everything that is part of a healthy fiscal and monetary system.

THE REAL pioneers today, those who are blazing a trail to the market economy, are our first entrepreneurs, who often must overcome unbelievable obstacles.

In the future society I am imagining, there will already be a very strong and powerful stratum, not just of small entrepreneurs, but also of middle-range and perhaps even large-scale entrepreneurs. The entrepreneurs will be the engine of our economic life, and will have the respect of society — which by this time will understand that ownership is not a vice, not something to be ashamed of, but rather a commitment, and an instrument by which the general good can be served.

The employee — and I would like to emphasize this especially, because we often forget about it — will be as respected as the entrepreneur or the employer. A firm's prosperity will depend as much on the people who work there as on the owner. Once this is recognized and accepted, people can feel that what they do and how they do it matters.

The previous regime presented itself as the government of the working class, yet it was able to make work such an anonymous process, and to obscure its value and significance so thoroughly, that workers lost something immensely important to everyone: the knowledge that their work meant something. The results of their work were dumped into the enormous pit of the unified state economy, and they had no idea whether their work made a contribution or was done utterly in vain. The workers, and in fact all citizens, became a single, enormous, anonymous body called "the masses" or "the working masses", a giant army of robots fulfilling quotas and plans, but with no control over the results of their work. True, work (or "honest work", as it was often called) was the subject of constant homilies by the regime, but in reality, respect for work declined. Work is always personal, and one does it well when one knows what it is for and what it will become — when one can take pride in it or know it will receive recognition. Only then can one enjoy work, and take a personal interest in what one does, the company one works for, the quality and outcome of one's efforts.

It may sound paradoxical to those brought up in the world of Communist ideology, but only with the renewal of the market economy, in which companies become legal entities under particular and responsible owner-ship, will respect for work be renewed as well. Diligence and skill will be recognized and rewarded; the self-esteem of all workers will be enhanced, and that includes all that goes with working-class self-esteem, such as working-class solidarity, the development of an authentic trade-union movement, the emergence of self-education movements, and the enrichment of the general culture.

In our case, something that could contribute to the self-esteem of employees and thus to the atmosphere of social peace would be — though I don't yet know to what extent — privatization via coupons, which citizens could purchase and convert to shares in newly privatized com-panies. This process would strengthen the perception that everyone had an equal chance. In a relatively simple way, and without needing access to capital, any employee could choose to become an "employer" — that is, a co-owner of some enterprise.

There will, of course, be unemployed people. I hope there will not, however, be more than is necessary and unavoidable in a market economy (3 per cent? 5 per cent?)

The state will support every measure by which unemployment can be dealt with, from the creation of new job opportunities and requalification programs, to commissioning work from private firms, to, in some cases, even investment in public works. All such measures are better than merely paying out unemployment insurance, not only because — directly or indirectly — they create new value, but also because of the distressing social and psychological consequences of living on unemployment insurance.

A GREAT transformation and rebirth are awaiting agriculture. As I write this, impassioned debates about its future are taking place. I often hear voices (frequently addressed to me) claiming that we are trying to destroy agriculture in this country, that we are disparaging the honest work of those who feed us and the great achievements of our "whole agribusiness". I do not disparage the honest work of these workers, because I do not disparage any honest work. I am certainly not interested in destroying our agriculture; on the contrary, I wish for its recovery. And so far, no one has convinced me that it is not seriously ailing.

The Communist regime, guided by the ideological doctrine of parity between rural and urban areas, treated agriculture as a single gigantic industrial plant, and turned farmers into employees. A system of enormous transfer payments kept rural areas relatively well off, as far as their standard of living went, but the price they paid was extensive proletarianization. Farm villages ceased to be true villages and became more like dormitory communities for agricultural labourers. Farmers were no longer close to their livestock or the soil. Animals were moved from pastures and well-kept stables laid with clean straw into vast factory barns where they stand in stalls on metal grates, often never seeing the sun or having the run of a meadow in their entire lives. These barns were painted with toxic disinfectant. The land was polluted with chemical fertilizers. Ploughing under the strips and hedgerows dividing the fields and introducing heavy machinery led to the destruction of the ecological balance, to erosion, and to the disintegration, compacting, and deadening of the soil, which in turn led to more excessive chemical fertilizing and the expensive liquidation of pests that would otherwise be eaten by the birds that had been driven from the fields. The yields are decent, it is true, but the produce is not of high quality, and the meat sometimes contains toxic substances. The absurd centralization (so-called wholesale production) and, in some places, unnatural specialization disproportionately increased the consumption of energy in agriculture. Farmers are dependent on the large and often monopolistic purchasing, processing, and distributing organizations that have them — and the distributors — completely in their hands. I don't want to overgeneralize. I know of prospering and ecologically conscientious cooperatives. Nevertheless, on the basis of my own observations, I think that on the whole the state of things is bad.

All of this must be changed, and it will obviously take years. I can imagine, however, that ten years from now this great rebirth of agriculture should be basically complete. It should definitely not rage through the land the way the whirlwind of collectivization in the 1950s did. But it should leave our countryside looking essentially different. First of all, our villages will once again have become villages, modern and pleasing to the eye. The natural connections between their traditional *raison d'être* — a place for people to live, for the raising of livestock, and for the cultivation of the fields — must be gradually renewed. Agriculture should once again be in the hands of the farmers — people who own the land, the meadows, the orchards, and the livestock, and take care of them. In part, these will be small farmers who have been given back what was taken from them; in part, larger family farms; and in part (and a large part, at that!) modest co-operatives of owners or commercial enterprises. The gigantic co-operative enterprises are not working, and should be divided and transformed.

A pluralistic network of processing and marketing co-operatives, to which farmers also belong, will exist. Private, co-op, and other enterprises for the rental of agricultural equipment will come into being. Other forms of ownership will undoubtedly also be created. Some of the unified fields — for instance, those in the Labe basin — are not worth dividing up into smaller farms again, unless the exigencies of the restitution process and the unwillingness of private owners to join together make it impossible to do otherwise. But in most places it would be reasonable to divide unified fields into smaller fields, separated once again by strips of grass and shrubbery.

Of course, the slaughterhouses, dairies, processing industries, and wholesale networks will all be privatized. The farmers themselves know best — and new farmers will quickly learn — how to renew the ecological balance, how to cultivate the soil and gradually bring it back to health. I also believe that a portion of the agricultural land should simply be left fallow, converted to pasture land, or reforested. We have few forests, while there is already, and probably will be in the future, a surplus of agricultural products.

A traditional scale and proportion should be restored to our environment, and we must renew the old connections between its elements. This concerns not only our once-picturesque countryside, woods, and fields, but also the farm buildings, the churches, chapels, and wayside crosses. I am not harbouring an antiquarian desire to return to the time of my youth, when work in the fields was incredible drudgery. I would be completely satisfied if, in ten years, our rural areas looked and functioned something like the rural areas in, for example, Denmark. I am continually shocked at how sharply our western border stands out, both from the air and from the ground. On one side of the border there are neat, well-kept fields, pathways, and orchards, and among them perfectly tended estates and farms. Every square metre — again! — is being used for something, and you can see in it evidence of human care, based on respect for the soil. On the other side there are extensive fields with crops lying unharvested on the ground, stockpiles of chemicals, unused land, land crisscrossed with tire tracks, neglected pathways, no rows of trees or woodlots. Villages are merely the remains of villages, interspersed with something that resembles factory yards or production halls. There is mud everywhere, and occasionally, like a fist in the face, an ugly new prefab apartment building, utterly out of place in a rural setting. At the same time, the countryside is set about with monstrous shiny silos painted with poison.

PERHAPS the most difficult thing of all will be the ecological revival of our land, its devastated countryside and polluted cities.

But even here — with a little imagination — we can see that in ten or fifteen years things could be essentially different. There should be, as I have said, an increase in woodlots, which will contribute to the amount of oxygen in the air. There should also be a decrease in sulphur dioxide and all harmful atmospheric emissions. The thermal-electricity generating plants that are not closed down will convert to clean combustion technology (I saw this working in Sweden), or will be provided with scrubbers and filters. Our overdeveloped and insanely concentrated chemical industry will, I hope, be brought under control. There are projects for saving the dying forests and for recultivating the destroyed countryside. But a little of the moonscape in northern Bohemia, with its open pit mines and dead trees, will still remain, since revitalizing it completely will take many decades.

Ecologists are already working on plans to regenerate our rivers and to treat effluent wastes. It makes no sense to build power sources and industries that destroy nature, the air, and the water, and then turn around and invest the profits in measures to rectify the damage. We must achieve a situation in which firms are compelled to choose alternatives that are ecologically sounder, though this may mean far higher initial investment. This cannot be done without the participation of the state, well-thought-out economic policies, and strict ecological laws. The state must systematically make use of all the means it has to compel companies to behave responsibly. If it does so, the results will certainly be visible in ten years.

Related to the transformation of our agriculture and the ecological policies of our government is the task of renewing the landscape in areas where agriculture and industry have destroyed it. That too requires a concept that is reflected in the choice of economic instruments; it need not simply take more money out of the state budget. The first traces of such an approach should be observable by the beginning of the next millennium.

WHAT will the international position of our country be?

If everything goes well, we will be full members of the European Community, we will have a firm place in the growing pan-European association, and we will have solid guarantees of our security, flowing from the security system that Europe will have developed by that time. In other words, we will have essentially built our new home in Europe. Our independence will have substance, meaning, and context. We will no longer feel naked, helpless, isolated, forgotten, and threatened.

Ján Čarnogurský often speaks about how Slovakia wants its own star on the future flag of Europe, and its own seat at the table. The European firmament is large and I see no reason why there shouldn't be two independent stars in it, Czech and Slovak, though from a distance they might look like a binary star. By the time the European Community has a firmly integrated political leadership, by the time we are part of its monetary union, by the time not only tourists but workers and capital are flowing freely across our borders, by the time those borders are only a formality and we are bound in many things by an integrated legislative system and have handed over many powers to supranational institutions or, instead, to individual regions — by that time the number of stars we have in the European flag will not seem as important as it may seem to some today.

Nevertheless, if our citizens wish it, they will have every right to change the number of stars on the flag; there will be far fewer obstacles, dangers, and problems involved in the division of our country in ten years than there are today. But this is all the more reason for thinking that, if separation is really what is meant by the demand for two stars, it is not very clever to emphasize it too strongly today. A country that declares its own existence as temporary, that reveals its disinclination to go on existing for much longer, will not enjoy a great deal of confidence. No partner is going to perceive us as solid and trustworthy, as a country that stands behind what it does because it is sure of its identity and is therefore responsible for itself. If we intend to defer separation for practical reasons, then for the same practical reasons we should defer any talk of separation.

Nations have their own identities — spiritual, intellectual, cultural, and political — which they reveal to the world each day through their actions. This is true as well of Czechs and of Slovaks. Our identity is something that other European countries have long recognized, and will continue to recognize through our everyday deeds. We should talk about any eventual changes in our identity as a state the moment we genuinely want to change it. After all, we will have a right to do so at any time.

MARXISTS considered everything that was not material production as its "superstructure". I personally have never agreed with a division of human affairs into what is primary and what is secondary. I've spent many years of my life participating in "material production", but I never had the feeling that my spirit, my intellect, my consciousness — in other words, what makes me a person — was somehow determined by that. On the contrary, if I produced something, I produced it as a person — that is, a creature with a spirit and a conscious mastery of his own fate. It was the outcome of a decision made by my human "I", and, to a greater or lesser extent, that "I" had to share in my material production.

In a way, what Marxists understand as social being really does determine social consciousness. In another way, however — and for me this is far more decisive — it is social consciousness that determines social being. Even Communism first had to be thought up; only afterwards could it be brought into existence.

If I have left my thoughts on what spiritual and intellectual life will be like at the beginning of the next century to the end of these reflections on the future, it is not because I perceive that life as a "superstructure". In fact, just the opposite is true: I want to talk about it last because it seems to me the most important.

All my observations and all my experience have, with remarkable consistency, convinced me that, if today's planetary civilization has any hope of survival, that hope lies chiefly in what we understand as the human spirit. If we don't wish to destroy ourselves in national, religious, or political discord; if we don't wish to find our world with twice its current population, half of it dying of hunger; if we don't wish to kill ourselves with ballistic missiles armed with atomic warheads or eliminate ourselves with bacteria specially cultivated for the purpose; if we don't wish to see some people go desperately hungry while others throw tons of wheat into the ocean; if we don't wish to suffocate in the global greenhouse we are heating up for ourselves or to be burned by radiation leaking through holes we have made in the ozone; if we don't wish to exhaust the non-renewable, mineral resources of this planet, without which we cannot survive; if, in short, we don't wish any of this to happen, then we must — as humanity, as people, as conscious beings with spirit, mind, and a sense of responsibility — somehow come to our senses.

I once called this coming to our senses an existential revolution. I meant a kind of general mobilization of human consciousness, of the human mind and spirit, human responsibility, human reason.

Perhaps, in light of this view, it makes sense that I cannot consider upbringing, education, and culture as mere ornaments to decorate and beautify life, and enrich our leisure time.

So how do I see our future in this sphere?

I hope it won't be taken as further proof of my crypto-socialism if I say that our state — regardless of how poor it may be — should not stint in cultivating its spiritual and intellectual life, in cultivating education. In the most advanced countries, government investment is directed first and foremost towards the development of education, science, and culture. Every crown the state invests in those fields will return to it a thousandfold, though the profit cannot be measured by standard accounting procedures.

The methods of achieving such cultivation will obviously be varied, and will correspond to market conditions. They will be subject to public control but will be separated, as far as possible, from the civil service, and designed to achieve maximum plurality. Along with grants, there will be charitable foundations, tax write-offs and relief, funds, grants, and so on.

THE MOST basic sphere of concern is schooling. Everything else depends on that.

What will our schools be like? I think that in ten years they should be fully reformed and consolidated. The point, understandably, is not just the reconstruction of school buildings or the supply of computers and new textbooks. The most important thing is a new concept of education. At all levels, schools must cultivate a spirit of free and independent thinking in the students. Schools will have to be humanized, both in the sense that their basic component must be the human personalities of the teachers, creating around themselves a "force field" of inspiration and example, and in the sense that technical and other specialized education will be balanced by a general education in the humanities.

The role of the schools is not to create "idiot-specialists" to fill the special needs of different sectors of the national economy, but to develop the individual capabilities of the students in a purposeful way, and to send out into life thoughtful people capable of thinking about the wider social, historical, and philosophical implications of their specialities. All those who today seriously and deeply concern themselves with scientific disciplines — from chemistry or mathematics, all the way to zootechnology — must somehow be touched by basic human questions such as the meaning of our being, the structure of space and time, the order of the universe, and the position of human existence in it. The schools must also lead young people to become self-confident, participating citizens; if everyone doesn't take an interest in politics, it will become the domain of those least suited to it.

The universities will not select students; everyone must have access to education. But all students must, at the same time, reckon with the fact that they may not pass muster; and even if they do, and finish their studies, their lives after that will be chiefly in their own hands. No one will guarantee them work in their field. The state will no longer regulate the admission of students and the employment of university graduates according to the needs of some five-year plan. The more citizens who complete university, the better. I do not see what harm it can do for a businessman, a restaurant owner, or an official of the state to have studied law.

Our universities will be decentralized and richly diversified. The recently established regional universities will be breathing more easily. Each school will develop its own speciality, something unique to attract students, such as a reputation for a high level of academic achievement in a particular discipline, an important scientific team, or a remarkable pedagogue or researcher who is known for his own "school".

Many of our students will complete their studies abroad, and then return and start teaching in our schools. Teachers from abroad will be welcomed to teach here as well, of course — something that is already happening.

SINCE time immemorial, a part of human culture has been man's care for himself, for the body in which the spirit resides — that is, for his own health. The culture of healing may be a less visible aspect of life, yet it is perhaps the most important indicator of the humanity of any society.

Therefore I pose this as my last question: what will our health-care services look like in this new world I'm trying to imagine?

A whole new health system should be built by then. It will be a liberal system, which means that patients and doctors will have a choice. State and university health facilities will be interconnected with local and private systems, and with systems run by churches and charities. A large proportion of doctors will have private practices, and this — among other things — will help to decentralize the health-care system. Hospitals, clinics, and the present national health institutes will also be partially privatized, with part remaining public, and part remaining under state ownership but leased to private practitioners and their teams. Getting medical care will no longer be the bureaucratic nightmare it has been for the past forty years.

Doctors will be paid for their services through a new system of general health insurance, and in some cases they'll be paid directly. If this prospect worries some people, let me remind them that health care is not free today: we all pay for it through our taxes. The difference is that until recently we didn't have any control over the money we paid out. (Who could tell how much of our taxes went to pay the dentist, and how much to build the Palace of Culture?) Nor did we have any say in the level of services provided. We will continue to pay for health service as we do today; the only difference will be that we will know precisely how much we are paying, to whom, for what, and why. Yet the health-insurance system will make up for the ironies of nature, through which a rich person may never be sick a day in his life and a poor person may require expensive heart operations.

The most important aspect of health care, however, is the

same as in everything else: the personal relationship between doctor and patient. People are not just racks on which to hang various organs — kidneys, stomach, and so on — that can be repaired by specialists, as you would repair a car. They are integral beings in whom every part is intimately interrelated, and in whom everything is mysteriously connected to the spirit. That is why we are best treated by a doctor to whom we are not just anonymous biological mechanisms, but individual, unique, and familiar human beings. In short, hospitals and doctors' offices will no longer be either state institutions that dispense prescriptions and certificates of incapacity, or state repair shops for broken-down robots. And it's not only patients who dream about the state of affairs I describe here; doctors long for it as well.

There is also much to be done in the area of care for the disabled. The state will offer incentives to enterprises that offer jobs to the disabled. They must be guaranteed the supportive devices they need. New homes must be built for the elderly and for mentally incapable children; such institutions are now in a shocking condition. Some of these functions may be taken over by the church, others will be undertaken by private institutions and foundations, yet others will be run by the community, and some will continue to be operated by the state. The main thing that must be changed, however, is our attitude to the physically and mentally handicapped. We have too often pretended they don't exist. We have looked on indifferently while they were pushed out to the margins of society.

I WILL not go on about my dreams and imaginings for all the areas that have little to do with material production, but without which a genuinely dignified human life on earth is unthinkable. I will only summarize what many wise people are thinking about every day, in far more specific terms than I can employ here.

All these areas have one thing in common: today, everything is in preparation: projects, concepts, draft legislation; in ten years or so, much of all that could well be realized. For the time being, the educational system, scientific research, the health service, social welfare, and culture are all badly off. Almost no one has any money for anything, and often the feeling prevails that everything is falling apart. In a way this is true. The former centralist, bureaucratic, and dysfunctional system of support for what cannot be self-supporting is collapsing. The new system, in all its aspects, is being born, prepared, thought through. But it is not yet up and working.

In ten years it will be working — it must be. It is vitally important for all of us that it should be. I have said on various occasions that none of the big problems in this country, from ecological, economic, and technical matters to political ones, will be resolved quickly and successfully if they are not undertaken by educated and cultivated people who are at the same time decent people. And the basic measure of the general state of decency is how a society cares for its children, its sick, its elderly, and its helpless. In other words, how it looks after its own.

The state is not something unconnected to society, hovering above or outside it, a necessary and anonymous evil. The state is a product of society, an expression of it, an image of it. It is a structure that a society creates for itself as an instrument of its own self-realization. If we wish to create a good and humane society, capable of making a contribution to humanity's "coming to its senses", we must create a good and humane state. That means a state that will no longer suppress, humiliate, and deny the free human being, but will serve all the dimensions of that being. That means a state that will not shift our hearts and minds into a special little niche labelled "superstructure", tolerated and developed for decorative purposes only.

Epilogue

TODAY we often hear the line "We needn't discover what has already been discovered! Why reinvent the wheel?" I understand this sentiment and I fully agree with it — most of the time. Indeed, it makes no sense to attempt to rediscover the law of supply and demand, the principle of shareholding or value-added tax, the basic constellation of human rights and freedoms, techniques of municipal self-government, tried and true elements of parliamentary democracy, or lead-free gasoline.

I even understand this sentiment when it means something broader, a more general message that might be formulated as: "Let us be done with the silly, inflated notion that Czechoslovakia is the navel of the world, capable of endowing humanity with a brand-new and unheard-of political and economic system, one that will take the world by storm." If the sentiment is a protest against the conceited idea that we alone are capable of inventing a better world, then again I can only concur. After all, it was I who long ago, back in 1968, made a lot of enemies by ridiculing the illusions of reform Communists that we were practically the most important country in the world because we were the first to try to combine socialism and democracy. These days, such objections are aimed at advocates of the so-called third way, which is meant to be some combination of capitalism and socialism. I don't know exactly how anyone understands this "third way", in specific terms, but if it is meant to refer to some combination of the unproven and the proven, I must place myself on the side of those who would rather not have anything to do with it.

But sometimes — especially in the hands of people with a tendency towards dogmatic, ideological thinking — this sentiment becomes a kind of hickory stick to crack across the knuckles of anyone who does not want, for whatever reason, to copy faithfully all the models presented — which today, of course, are western models. If that is what it means, then I can't agree. Without being, as I have said, a seeker after some "third way", I am opposed to blind imitation, especially if it becomes an ideology. My reason for this is very simple: it is against nature and against life. We will never turn Czechoslovakia into a Federal Republic of Germany, or a France, or a Sweden, or a United States of America, and I don't see the slightest reason why we should try. That would only raise the question of why we should be an independent country at all. Why bother learning such unimportant languages as Czech and Slovak in school? Why not apply at once to be the fifty-first state of the U.S.A.?

Life and the world are as beautiful and interesting as they are because, among other things, they are varied, because every living creature, every community, every country, every nation has its own unique identity. France is different from Spain and Spain is not the same as Finland. Each country has its own geographical, social, intellectual, cultural, and political climate. It is proper that things should be this way, and I cannot understand why we alone should be so ashamed of ourselves that we don't want to be Czechoslovakia. To me, this is like going from one extreme to another: one moment we take on the role of a world messiah; the next we are deeply ashamed of our very existence. (This, of course, is nothing new: we have experienced these swings from pomposity to masochism and back many times.)

To sum up: though we haven't the slightest reason not to learn from any place in the world that can offer us useful knowledge, at the same time I see no reason why we should be ashamed of trying to find our own way, one that derives from our Czechoslovak identity. In many cases we haven't really any choice. We are not doing this to dazzle the world with our originality, or to cure some inferiority complex. We are doing it purely and simply because it is the only possible way: our country is where it is, its landscape is beautiful in certain ways and devastated in others, its natural resources and industries are structured in such-and-such a way, we speak the languages we speak, we have our own historical traditions and customs, the political right and left are the way they are here and not the way they are elsewhere, and no matter how much we might want to, we can scarcely hope to change these things entirely. Why not accept all this as fact? Why not try to understand the inner content of this fact, the potential, the problems and hopes connected with it? And why not deal with it in the most appropriate and adequate way?

HAVING SAID that we must build a state based on intellectual and spiritual values, I must now touch on the question of what our intellectual and spiritual potential is, and whether it has any distinctive features at all. But to do that, I had first to come to terms with the possible accusation that I was seeking for our country something as shameful as its "own way".

Yes, our intellectual and spiritual potential really does have its own identity. We are what history has made us. We live in the very centre of Central Europe, in a place that from the beginning of time has been the main European crossroads of every possible interest, invasion, and influence of a political, military, ethnic, religious, or cultural nature. The intellectual and spiritual currents of east and west, north and south, Catholic and Protestant, enlightened and romantic — the political movements of conservative and progressive, liberal and socialist, imperialist and national liberationist — all of these overlapped here, and bubbled away in one vast cauldron, combining to form our national and cultural consciousness, our traditions, the social models of our behaviour, which have been passed down from generation to generation. In short, our history has formed our experience of the world.

For centuries, we — Czechs and Slovaks, whether in our own state or under foreign control — lived in a situation of constant menace from without. We are like a sponge that has gradually absorbed and digested all kinds of intellectual and cultural impulses and initiatives. Many European initiatives were born or first formulated here. At the same time, our historical experience has imbued us with a keen sensitivity to danger, including danger on a global scale. It has even made us somewhat prescient: many admonitory visions of the future — Kafka's and Čapek's, for instance — have come from here — and not by chance. The ethnic variety of this area, and life under foreign hegemony, have created different mutations of our specific Central European provinciality, which have frequently, and in very curious ways, merged with that clairvoyance.

Our most recent great experience, an experience none of the western democracies has ever undergone, was Communism. Often we ourselves are unable to appreciate fully the existential dimension of this bitter experience and all its consequences, including those that are entirely metaphysical. It is up to us alone to determine what value we place on that particular capital.

It is no accident that here, in this milieu of unrelenting danger, with the constant need to defend our own identity, the idea that a price must be paid for truth, the idea of truth as a moral value, has such a long tradition. That tradition stretches from Saints Cyril and Methodius, who brought

Christianity to the region in the ninth century A.D., through the fifteenth-century reformer Jan Hus, all the way down to modern politicians like Tomáš Garrigue Masaryk and Milan Štefánik, and the philosopher Jan Patočka.

When we think about all this, the shape of our present intellectual and spiritual character starts to appear — the outlines of an existential, social, and cultural potential which is slumbering here and which — if understood and evaluated — can give the spirit, or the idea, of our new state a unique and individual face.

Every European country has something particular to it — and that makes its autonomy worth defending, even in the framework of an integrating Europe. That autonomy then enriches the entire European scene; it is another voice in that remarkable polyphony, another instrument in that orchestra. And I feel that our historical experience, our intellectual and spiritual potential, our experience of misery, absurdity, violence, and idyllic tranquillity, our humour, our experience of sacrifice, our love of civility, our love of truth and our knowledge of the many ways truth can be betrayed — all this can, if we wish, create another of those distinct voices from which the chorus of Europe is composed.

We must learn wherever we can. But we can also offer something: not only the inimitable climate of our mind and spirit, not only the message we have mined from our historical experience, but — God willing — perhaps even an original way of breathing this character and experience into the newly laid foundations of our state, into the architecture of its institutions and the features of its culture.

Our great, specific experience of recent times is the collapse of an ideology. We have all lived through its tortured and complicated vagaries, and we have gone through it, as it were, to the bitter end. This experience has, to an extraordinary degree, strengthened my ancient skepticism towards all ideologies. I think that the world of ideologies and doctrines is on the way out for good — along with the entire modern age. We are on the threshold of an era of globality, an era of open society, an era in which ideologies will be replaced by ideas.

Building an intellectual and spiritual state — a state based on ideas — does not mean building an ideological state. Indeed, an ideological state cannot be intellectual or spiritual. A state based on ideas is precisely the opposite: it is meant to extricate human beings from the straitjacket of ideological interpretations, and to rehabilitate them as subjects of individual conscience, of individual thinking backed up by experience, of individual responsibility, and with a love for their neighbours that is anything but abstract.

A state based on ideas should be no more and no less than a guarantee of freedom and security for people who know that the state and its institutions can stand behind them only if they themselves take responsibility for the state — that is, if they see it as their own project and their own home, as something they need not fear, as something they can — without shame — love, because they have built it for themselves.

Afterword

A S FOR myself. . . .
The period when my entering the presidency merely climaxed the revolution is passing irretrievably into history. The era of opposition intellectuals in political office is passing away as well. It was a crucial moment in history when there were no professional democratic politicians, and the intellectuals had to fill in for them. Now an era is fast approaching that will belong to those who truly want to devote themselves to the practice of politics, permanently and with all their being, and who are prepared to fight for their political positions.

My political career too was, in the beginning, just a "filling in", something for which I personally feel little need, and which I see more as a burden than as a delight. What am I to do in this situation?

It would seem that only now has the time come for a really serious decision. Should I return to work as a writer? Or should I remain in practical politics and let my name stand once more for the presidential office?

I have been thinking about this decision for a long time, and it presents me with a genuine dilemma. There are so many arguments for and against.

The longer I think about it, the more clearly I come to realize that this dilemma is essentially just a new and particularly acute form of the same one I have faced throughout my adult life. Should I put myself and my personal interests first? That is, should I put the tranquil, less public, and certainly less exhausting life of an independent intellectual first? Or should I listen to the voice of "higher responsibility", which is constantly whispering in my ear that the work is far from done and that it is my duty to continue?

So far, whenever confronted with a decision of this kind, I have always decided in favour of struggling for commonly held values rather than taking the more comfortable way out. Why, therefore, should I not remain faithful to my own tradition? The condition and future of my country are not matters of indifference to me, and never will be. I have my own notions of what should be done, my own vision of a better state of things. I would have a hard time suppressing the feeling of obligation I have to struggle for my ideals. And so I say to myself: why hesitate? What is there to think about?

I don't mean to say that I want to run for president whatever the cost and whatever the circumstances, or even that I want to struggle to hold onto the office. (I have never fought for any position of power, and I'm not about to start now; it goes against my nature.) I am simply saying that, as a citizen, I will not let myself rest.

Time will show where I am best able to serve my own ideas, and where that opportunity will arise. The fact is — to put it somewhat disrespectfully — it's a secondary matter for me. The essential part is the values I espouse. I have already served them (with varying degrees of success) in many places: long ago as a member of the Writers' Union, briefly on radio after the Soviet occupation in 1968, later as a spokesman for Charter 77, then in prison, and ultimately as president. Perhaps I'll be able to serve them again as president, perhaps as an independent writer. But since I'm fated not to let myself rest, I mustn't rule out any possibilities in advance — even less so because the work is difficult. Therefore I can't rule out the possibility that I will run for office again.

For the time being, the possibility is truly only theoretical.

How many different conditions would first have to be fulfilled?

In the first place, someone would have to want me as president. What if, in the meantime, the public turns against me, either justifiably, because of some unforgivable mistake I might make, or for no particular reason, because people just long for a change?

It will depend even more on the political parties. It is hard to say whether they will want me, or whether Parliament will offer the post to someone more to their liking. Most of all, of course, it will depend on the parliamentary election and who wins it. It may be a coalition of parties that will not want to govern with me; or it may be parties that I, on the other hand, would not want to work with. Perhaps the disinclination will be mutual.

But it will depend on other things too. I am certainly not interested in being the president of a divided country, or a merely ceremonial president, someone who lays flowers at monuments and attends gala suppers. Were the president to be a figurehead, I dare say I could be far more useful to my country somewhere else, whether in the theatre, the press, or some benevolent organization.

But it doesn't only depend on others, it depends on me as well. What if I conclude that I am no longer up to the job, that I am making errors in judgement, that my work as president is not successful? I am more critical of myself than I let on, and I can't rule out that possibility.

In short, there are many factors to be taken into account. And so I can no longer say for certain any more than I've already said:

1) That I will not — even if it makes me different from all the other presidents in the world — fight to retain my position. I cannot imagine doing that.

2) That I will not give up certain values that I as a citizen believe in, but that I will always fight for them, regardless of what it is I happen to be doing.

3) That if circumstances combine to make my candidacy possible, and if I feel it makes sense — that is, if I feel I could work for my "civil program" best as president — then I am prepared to assume that burden for a third time.

For reasons I don't think I have to explain, it has not been easy for me to arrive at this apparently simple and logical position. But since I have worked it out, I think it only right that I say so, and say it at the end of this book, as an addendum to what is in it.

May God be with us.

Background Notes

by Paul Wilson

The following notes are keyed to words, phrases, or names in the text.

p. xiii: Pavel Tigrid. Czech journalist, author, and editor. Tigrid left Czechoslovakia after the Communist coup in 1948, and from the mid-fifties on he published *Svědectví*, an émigré quarterly which quickly became the journal of record for Czechoslovak affairs at home and abroad. He is now an adviser to President Havel.

p. xv: "Civic Forum and the Public Against Violence". Both groups were created in late November 1989 (the former in the Czech lands of Bohemia and Moravia, with roughly two-thirds of the population of fifteen and a half million, the latter in Slovakia) as umbrella organizations to guide the country through the complex process of wresting political power from the Communist Party. They rapidly became loosely organized, grass-roots movements and, in the elections of June 1990, each ran as a political party in its respective republic. Civic Forum got over 50 per cent of the popular vote in the Czech Republic, and the Public Against Violence about 35 per cent in the Slovak Republic. Since then, however, the Civic Forum has split into two different political parties (see note for p. 57, below). Like Civic Forum, the Public Against Violence also split into two different parties: the Movement for a Democratic Slovakia, led by Vladimír

Mečiar, and the Public Against Violence, led by Martin Porubjak. The former party favours a loose association between the Czech and Slovak republics, a slower pace of economic reform, and a greater degree of government involvement in the economy. As of February 1992 this party enjoyed a wide measure of popular support in Slovakia, standing at about 33 per cent in the polls. The Public Against Violence, which favours a strong federation and rapid economic reforms, is smaller and so far enjoys much less support, at around 6 per cent. According to the Czechoslovak election law, any party must poll at least 5 per cent of the popular vote to be represented in Parliament.

p. xvi: "'pulled forward by Being'". Havel frequently uses the capitalized expression "Being" both in his writing and in his public speeches. He explains at length what he means by the expression in many passages of his *Letters to Olga*. One example: "Behind all phenomena and discrete entities in the world, we may observe, intimate, or experience existentially in various ways something like a general 'order of Being'. The essence and meaning of this order are veiled in mystery; it is as much an enigma as the Sphinx, it always speaks to us differently and always, I suppose, in ways that we ourselves are open to, in ways, to put it simply, that we can hear." (Letter 76, pp. 185–86.) See also p. 6: "'the memory of Being'", and p. 62: "the order of Being".

Politics, Morality, and Civility

p. 3:   "*nomenklatura*". The Communist Party had a special elite membership category called the *nomenklatura*; only members of this elite were eligible to fill key positions in government, the bureaucracy, and the economy. There is widespread concern throughout Central and Eastern Europe and the former Soviet Union that people from the *nomenklatura*, with their accumulated wealth and their connections, are getting a head start in the new market economy. (See also p. 68.)

p. 5: "Charter 77". The human rights movement begun by Havel and many others in 1976 was launched in January 1977 (hence, the name — Charter 77) and quickly became the major focus in Czechoslovakia of peaceful dissident activities of all kinds. Havel, several times a Charter 77 spokesman, has written many commentaries on the movement's activities. For a detailed account of the origins, purposes, and activities of Charter 77, see H. Gordon Skilling's study *Charter 77 and Human Rights in Czechoslovakia* (London: George Allen & Unwin, 1981).

p. 6: "'higher' responsibility". Havel explains this notion at some length in the last sixteen letters in his *Letters to Olga* (New York: Alfred A. Knopf; London: Faber and Faber, 1988).

p. 6: "'the memory of Being'". See note for p. xvi, above.

p. 9: "'Conversations from Lány'". Almost every Sunday afternoon since he assumed office, Havel has gone on the air and talked to the nation about current issues. The talks are in the form of interviews, and are usually recorded at Lány, the presidential retreat, about thirty kilometres west of Prague.

In a Time of Transition

p. 21: "our three parliaments". The present Czechoslovak parliamentary system was inherited from the previous regime in 1989 and remains virtually intact. The country is a federation with strong central government and, though the Czech and Slovak republics each have their own representative bodies (the Czech National Council and the Slovak National Council) and their own governments, these bodies have less autonomy than provincial, state, or regional governments do in other federal systems, such as that of Canada and the United States. The federal Parliament is a bicameral body: the Assembly of the People is a 150-seat chamber, with 101 seats for the Czechs and 49 seats for the Slovaks; the Assembly of Nations has 150 seats, 75 for representatives from the Czech lands of Bohemia and Moravia and 75 for those from Slovakia. Voting in the Assembly of Nations is carried out by nationality; legislation has to be passed by a majority in each half of the house.

p. 23: "a prolonged struggle over the name of our country". Havel is referring here to what is sometimes called "the hyphen war" — a debate in Parliament, lasting from January to April 1990, about what the country should be called. Under the Communists, the country's official name had been the Czechoslovak Socialist Republic, or ČSSR. The original idea was simply to drop the word "socialist", but the discussion soon broadened to include two other alternatives: the original name, "Czechoslovakia", or a hyphenated version of the name, "Czecho-Slovakia" (sometimes used by non-Czech nationalists before the Second World War) that would give equal billing, as it were, to the Slovaks. After three months, a compromise was arrived at, and the official name of the country is now the Czech and Slovak Federal Republic, or ČSFR. "Czechoslovakia", however, still survives in popular usage.

p. 26: "Throughout their history — with the single infamous exception of the Slovak State . . . — they have always been ruled from elsewhere." The history of Slovak nationalism goes back to the nineteenth century, when Slovakia belonged to the Hungarian part of the Austro-Hungarian Empire, and Slovaks were on the receiving end of a policy of Hungarianization. When that empire collapsed after the First World War, both Czechs and Slovaks sought support for a common Czechoslovak state, although many Slovaks were hoping for a larger measure of autonomy within that state, including their own legislature, legal and financial institutions, and language rights (Slovak is a separate language). But the first president, Tomáš Garrigue Masaryk (see note for p. 127, below), favoured a "unitary state", that is, a single nation consisting of two peoples, rather than a true federation in which each nation has its own government. The first Czechoslovak constitution of 1920 reflected this unitary idea; Slovakia had virtually no autonomy, and the only constitutional means of satisfying Slovak political aspirations was to encourage Slovak participation in the central government. In addition, the Czech-dominated central government introduced policies of administrative reform that reinforced Prague centralism and were overtly assimilationist in their aims.

The friction and dissatisfaction that this arrangement caused in Slovakia fed the forces of nationalism and separatism, and on the eve of the outbreak of the Second World War, the separatist, Nazi-influenced Slovak People's Party, led by Monseigneur Tiso, was compelled by Hitler to declare independence. The independent Slovak state was established on March 14, 1939, a day before the rump of Bohemia and Moravia was occupied by German troops. It lasted until the end of the war. In the brief interim between the end of the war and the Communist take-over in 1948, the Slovaks enjoyed a measure of decreasing self-government, exercised through the Slovak National Council. Communist rule ended this. In 1968, during the period of liberalization under Alexander Dubček, himself a Slovak, the discussion of granting increased powers to

Slovakia was opened again, and, in fact, a new constitution that allowed for joint Czech and Slovak control
in some areas was drawn up and came into effect on
January 1, 1969. But with the Communist Party in
virtual control of all levels of government, such conces-
sions were hollow. This is what Havel refers to on p. 27
as "totalitarian federalization". During the 1970s and
1980s, even these tenuous powers were whittled away
by the forces of centralism.

p. 30:   "'natural world'". For a more complete account of
what Havel means by this expression, see his essay
"Politics and Conscience", in *Open Letters* (New York:
Alfred A. Knopf; London: Faber and Faber, 1991).
There, Havel talks about children and peasants being
"far more rooted in what some philosophers call 'the
natural world', or *Lebenswelt*, than most modern
adults. They have not yet grown alienated from the
world of their actual personal experience, the world
which has its morning and its evening, its *down* (the
earth) and its *up* (the heavens), where the sun rises
daily in the east, traverses the sky and sets in the west,
and where concepts like 'at home' and 'in foreign
parts', good and evil, beauty and ugliness, near and
far, duty and rights, still mean something living and
definite." (p. 250)

p. 30:   Jan Patočka (1907–1977). A philosopher and student
of Husserl and Heidegger, Patočka, along with Havel,
was one of the first three spokesmen for Charter 77
(see note for p. 5, above). In essays and lectures,
Patočka provided the philosophical underpinning
for the kind of civic activism represented by Charter
77. Havel has written a moving memoir of Patočka
called "Last Conversation", published in H. Gordon
Skilling's *Charter 77 and Human Rights in Czechoslovakia*,
pp. 242–44.

p. 38:   "the Czech republic would not accept an offer of confederation from Slovakia". Although the word "confederation" has been accorded many shades of meaning by countries with divergent historical experiences, Havel uses the word here to mean a voluntary association of otherwise independent states founded on the basis of a common treaty. From the point of view of international law, in Havel's understanding, members of a confederation are recognized as independent states, whereas a federation is recognized as a single state created from regions that retain a degree of autonomy but are under the authority of a single supreme law or constitution. Confusion may arise because some countries that call themselves confederations (Canada and Switzerland, for instance) are, by this definition, really federations.

p. 43:   Ján Čarnogurský (1944–). A lawyer and former dissident who served briefly in the first non-Communist government formed after the collapse of Communist rule in 1989. He is now the premier of Slovakia and head of the Christian Democratic Movement of Slovakia (KDHS). He is one of the chief proponents of a Czech and Slovak confederation.

p. 46:   "'minority veto'". The Czech term I have translated with this phrase is "*zakaz majorizace*", which literally means the capacity to overrule a majority vote. This describes a provision whereby the Slovak half of the Assembly of Nations can block certain legislation otherwise passed by a majority in the Assembly of the People. (See note to p. 21, above, for a fuller description of the Czechoslovak bicameral system.) Since the power to stop, or veto, certain legislation in effect belongs to the Slovak bloc in the Assembly of Nations, I have chosen an interpretative, rather than a literal, translation of the Czech phrase. Eyebrows may be raised, but I stand by my decision.

p. 48: "the Public Against Violence". See note to p. xv, above.

p. 49: "our present constitution still in fact assumes that leading role [of the Communist Party]". The clause guaranteeing the Communist Party's "leading role" was struck from the Czechoslovak constitution in late November 1989, in answer to one of the Civic Forum's basic demands. Under Communist rule, that clause had effectively placed the party above the constitution and turned the traditional elements of government — the legislature, the executive, and the judiciary — into instruments of party power, thus eliminating the need for constitutional provisions for a breakdown in government.

p. 54: Ferdinand Peroutka (1895–1978). One of the most highly respected political journalists in Czechoslovakia. During the Second World War he was interned in Buchenwald, and after the Communist *putsch* in 1948 he emigrated to the west, where he helped found Radio Free Europe. In the mid-1950s, he moved to New York, where he spent the remainder of his life. *The Building of a State* is one of his major works, and chronicles the creation of an independent Czechoslovakia, from 1917 to 1923.

p. 56: Petr Pithart (1941–). Political scientist and sociologist who was active in the reform process of 1968 and later in Charter 77 (see note to p. 5, above). After the Velvet Revolution, he became premier of the Czech Republic. He is a member of the Civic Movement (OH). Pithart is also author of a study of the Prague Spring called *Nineteen Sixty-eight — Osmašedesátý* (Prague: Rozmluvy, 1990).

p. 56: Josef Vavroušek (1944–). Environmentalist and systems analyst active in the Civic Forum (see note to p. xv, above) in 1989, he is now the federal minister of the environment.

p. 56–7: The passage on Havel's proposed changes to the electoral laws has been slightly amplified for clarity.

p. 57: Václav Klaus (1941–). Economist, federal minister of finance since December 1989. Also head of the Civic Democratic Party (ODS).

p. 57: Jiří Dienstbier (1937–). Former journalist and activist in Charter 77 (see note to p. 5, above); minister of foreign affairs since December 1989. He is head of the Civic Movement (OH).

p. 57: Vladimír Dlouhý (1953–). Economist; served as deputy prime minister and chairman of the Planning Commission from December 1989 until June 1990, when he became federal minister of the economy. He is a leading member of the Civic Democratic Alliance (ODA).

p. 57: Josef Lux (1956–). Chairman of the Czechoslovak People's Party.

The first three of the above men were all members of Civic Forum from its inception in November 1989. Havel's point is that since they were all members of the same party, they could have, theoretically, all run in the same district and, under the proportional system, people could have elected all of them simply by voting for the Civic Forum list. In February 1991, however, the Civic Forum split into two parties, the left-of-centre Civic Movement (OH) and the right-of-centre Civic Democratic Party (ODS). Vladimír

Dlouhý founded a third party, the Civic Democratic Alliance (ODA). Under the proportional system, the voter will now have to choose among them. Under Havel's proposed system, described on p. 57, the voter could give a favoured candidate a preferential vote, regardless of the candidate's party affiliation.

p. 59:   The entire contents of this page are new to this edition.

What I Believe

p. 61:   "I once said that I considered myself a socialist". See "'It Always Makes Sense to Tell the Truth': An Interview with Jiří Lederer", in Václav Havel, *Open Letters*, p. 97. For a more complete analysis of the word "socialism", see Havel's address "A Word About Words", in *Open Letters*, pp. 377–89.

p. 62:   "the order of Being". See note for p. xvi, above.

p. 65:   "marketing crisis". Havel is referring here to more than just the loss of traditional markets within the Soviet system (see note for Comecon, p. 74, below). Many companies have not been quick enough to adapt to new market conditions in which the patterns of demand are changing and competition is emerging. Domestic demand for some types of goods has been seriously weakened by inflation and wage restraints. Some manufacturers have sold large inventories of goods on credit and have not been paid. All these factors contribute to the "crisis" Havel talks about here.

p. 68:   "*nomenklatura*". See note for p. 3, above.

p. 72:   Gabčikovo Dam. A Czechoslovak-Hungarian mega-project (partly financed by Austria) in which the

Danube River below Bratislava is being dammed and rechannelled to produce hydroelectric power. It has been under way for more than a decade and has been the target of increasing environmental criticism in both countries. In 1991, the Hungarian side withdrew under pressure from ecological activists. Although the Czechoslovak government was also opposed to the project (Havel called it "a scar on the face of Europe"), it is too far advanced simply to abandon. Czechoslovakia has decided to go ahead with it, and is now trying to compel the Hungarian government to live up to its side of the agreement.

p. 72: The Temelín nuclear power facility is at present under construction near the village of Temelín in South Bohemia. Work was begun in 1984 and is scheduled for gradual completion this decade. Although once a focus, like the Gabčikovo Dam project, of environmental protests, there is no longer any serious opposition to its construction. Everyone seems to have conceded that this is the only way to phase out the coal-burning thermal-electricity plants in North Bohemia that are still creating serious pollution problems.

p. 74: The Council for Mutual Economic Assistance — Comecon. A Soviet organization that was responsible for co-ordinating economic policy in the satellite states of Eastern Europe. When it was established in 1949, Comecon was supposed to be a Soviet response to the Marshall Plan, which provided desperately needed aid to countries devastated by the war. Later, Comecon became an instrument for imposing structural changes on the economies of the satellites and, from 1968 until its gradual collapse after 1989, it worked to organize trade both within the Soviet bloc and between the bloc and the rest of the world. It was officially dissolved on June 28, 1991, in Budapest.

The Task of Independence

p. 81: Miloš Jakeš. Jakeš became First Secretary of the Communist Party in December 1987, succeeding Gustav Husák (who stayed on as president). He stepped down on November 24, 1989, a few days after the Velvet Revolution had got under way. He had little understanding of or sympathy for the politics of *perestroika* and may have been, as Havel suggests, an embarrassment to the Soviets. There is even a theory that the events of November 17, 1989, when the brutal suppression of a student demonstration set the changes in motion, were engineered by reform-minded Communists to bring about Jakeš's downfall.

p. 85: The paragraph beginning "The momentous changes in the Soviet Union" to the end of the section on page 86, contains new material from my interview with Havel.

p. 85: Nagorno-Karabakh. An autonomous region on the territory of Azerbaijan populated largely by ethnic Armenians. There has been open warfare between Armenia and Azerbaijan over the territory since 1990.

p. 87: The Council of Europe. Founded in 1949, the Council has its headquarters in Strasbourg, but is organizationally separate from the European Community. It consists of a Committee of Ministers, a Consultative Assembly, and a European Court of Human Rights. It has limited powers, and meetings of the Assembly serve mainly as a forum for discussion on matters of common interest.

p. 88–9: "The civil war in Yugoslavia". The two paragraphs on Yugoslavia have been added from the interview.

p. 90: "President François Mitterrand's initiative". This conference was seen by some as an attempt by the French to create an association of "second-class" European countries that would appear to give them a voice, but, in effect, would slow down their entry into the European Community. The Czechoslovak side, however, saw it as a positive step that could, in fact, accelerate their acceptance by the EC.

p. 93: The paragraph beginning "The CSCE will also intensify and deepen its work" contains new material from my interview with Havel.

p. 95: "the Munich Agreement of 1938". An agreement reached at a conference in Munich on September 29, 1938, between Hitler and the prime ministers of Britain, France, and Italy to cede the Sudetenland — comprising half the territory of Bohemia and 4.5 million of its people, most of whom were ethnic Germans — to Germany. A year later, when war broke out anyway, it became a vivid symbol of the folly of appeasement. (For a clear account of the events leading up to the Munich Agreement, see A.H. Hermann, *A History of the Czechs* [London: Allen Lane, 1975].)

The present Czechoslovak position is that the Munich Agreement was null and void from the beginning because it was signed under threat of force. Of the original signatories, only Great Britain declined to declare it retroactively null and void — "clearly," says one Czech official, "not to create a precedent for other agreements that it concluded in the past as a colonial power." The Germans were also reluctant to nullify the Munich Agreement because of domestic legal considerations. As a result, the treaty, as signed in Prague on February 27, 1992, does not contain an explicit "Munich paragraph", although it does recognize a treaty signed in Prague in 1973 that, in terms of international law, does *de facto* nullify it.

p. 95–7: Some of the material on the bilateral agreements, especially concerning the Soviet Union, has been brought up to date for this edition.

p. 96: "a conciliatory offer to the Sudeten Germans". After the Second World War ended, the Czechoslovak government expelled (or "transferred" — there is a debate over the proper term) almost two million Sudeten Germans to Germany, at the same time confiscating their property. The surviving Sudetenlanders are now lobbying to get their property back, but Czechoslovak law provides for the restitution of only that property confiscated by the Communists after February 1948. During his term of office, Havel has consistently sought to defuse the issue with candour. On his first official visit to Germany as president in January 1990, he risked disfavour at home by apologizing for the expulsion of the Germans, an apology he reiterated on the eve of signing the new treaty. And on a visit to Bonn in May 1991, Havel suggested that, although their property could not be returned, the Sudetenlanders could be given Czechoslovak citizenship and allowed to take part in the privatization process.

p. 96: Henleinians. Followers of Konrad Henlein (1898–1945), who was leader of the Sudeten Germans and used by Hitler to engineer the annexation of the Sudetenland to the German Reich in 1938. Henlein committed suicide in 1945 to avoid execution.

Beyond the Shock of Freedom

p. 102: "Political life will have become more harmonious". At present, there are seventy-eight registered political parties in the Czech lands, and eighty in Slovakia. Havel's hope is that, with a majority electoral system, this number will be drastically reduced.

p. 103: "an ample supply of new judges". Under Communist rule the judiciary was the handmaiden of party policy. In the transitional period Havel is writing about, it has been difficult to find judges who are not compromised by their past and can be trusted to hand down independent decisions.

p. 111: "unified fields". Until 1948, private farm fields in Czechoslovakia were often divided by hedgerows or strips of grass. When the Communists collectivized the farms in the 1950s, these hedgerows and grass medians were ploughed under and the individual plots were "unified" into large fields run by the state farms. Their restitution to the private sphere is a special problem.

p. 112: "insanely concentrated chemical industry". Havel is referring to the large pockets of chemical factories and refineries, mainly in northern and eastern Bohemia, but elsewhere as well, that are, along with the thermal-electricity plants, responsible for most of the serious pollution in these regions.

p. 113: "the moonscape in northern Bohemia". Most of the brown coal in north Bohemia is recovered through open pit mining, which has devastated large tracts of the countryside. As well, many of the forested areas in the northwest have been killed by emissions from the thermal-electricity plants that burn the coal, and from the chemical factories.

p. 114: Ján Čarnogurský. See note to p. 43, above.

Epilogue

p. 126: "European initiatives". Havel here means ideas for or attempts to create some form of organization that would transcend ethnic or national communities. He may have had in mind people like King Jiří of Poděbrady, who tried, in the fifteenth century, to establish a council of European monarchs, or the efforts of the second Czechoslovak president, Edvard Beneš, to establish Czechoslovakia's position as a bridge between east and west.

p. 126: "admonitory visions". Havel could have been thinking of many things here, from the legend of the Golem, through the works of Franz Kafka (1883–1924), which foreshadow the alienating and absurd world of totalitarian bureaucracy, to the plays and novels of Karel Čapek (1890–1938), who, in his play *R.U.R.*, coined the word "robot", and who warned of the grave dangers of totalitarianism in such works as *War with the Newts* (a novel) and *The White Plague* (a play).

p. 126: Cyril (827–869) and Methodius (826–885). Two brothers who, at the invitation of King Rastislav of Great Moravia, brought Christianity to the Central European Slavs in 863. Through translations of scripture lessons and liturgical offices into the vernacular, they introduced to the region a modified form of the Greek alphabet, the modern form of which (Cyrillic) is still used in parts of Yugoslavia, in Bulgaria, and in the former Soviet Union.

p. 127: Jan Hus (1372–1415). A religious reformer, influenced partly by the ideas of John Wycliffe. He was appointed Rector of Prague University in 1409. For his sermons and his criticism of the Church, he was excommunicated and then burned at the stake. He also simplified Czech orthography, introducing the systematic use of diacritical marks that make Czech spelling virtually phonetic. Hus's teachings and example have been an inspiration to the Czechs throughout their history, and his dictum "The truth prevails" was incorporated in the presidential standard and the official seal of the republic by Tomáš Garrigue Masaryk (see below).

p. 127: Tomáš Garrigue Masaryk (1850–1937). The first Czechoslovak president, who led the movement for Czech and Slovak independence from the Austro-Hungarian Empire, and finally achieved it in 1918. Masaryk is still revered today as a man who, in his writing and by his example, provided high standards of conduct for the whole country to aspire to.

p. 127: Milan Rastislav Štefánik (1880–1919). A Slovak astronomer and pilot in the French air force, Štefánik joined Masaryk and Beneš in France during the First World War and became co-founder of the Czechoslovak National Council. He travelled widely throughout Europe, helping to build up international support for the cause of Czechoslovak independence. Štefánik died tragically in a plane crash on his return to the country in 1919.

p. 127: Jan Patočka. See note for p. 30, above.

p. 130: "Charter 77". See note to p. 5, above.

A NOTE ABOUT THE AUTHOR
AND THE TRANSLATOR

Václav Havel was born in Czechoslovakia in 1936. Among his plays are *The Garden Party, The Memorandum, Largo Desolato, Temptation,* and three one-act plays, *Audience, Private View,* and *Protest.* He is a founding spokesman of Charter 77 and the author of many influential essays on totalitarianism and dissent. In 1979, he was sentenced to four and a half years in prison for his involvement in the Czech human rights movement; out of this came his book of letters to his wife, *Letters to Olga* (1988). In November 1989, he helped found the Civic Forum, a movement that negotiated the Communists out of power. From 1989 to 1992, he was president of Czechoslovakia, and in January 1993, he was elected president of the Czech Republic.

Paul Wilson lived in Czechoslovakia from 1967 to 1977. Since his return to Canada in 1978, he has translated into English work by many Czech writers, including Josef Škvorecký, Bohumil Hrabal, and Ivan Klíma. He has also translated and edited most of Václav Havel's prose writings to appear in English, including *Letters to Olga* (1988), *Disturbing the Peace* (1990), and *Open Letters* (1991). He lives in Toronto, where he works as a freelance writer and translator. He is a research associate at the Centre for Russian and Eastern European Studies in Toronto.

DISTURBING THE PEACE

A national bestseller—a witty, probing and eloquent work that is at once Havel's political autobiography, a history of Czechoslovakia under communism, a meditation on the social and political role of art, and a guide for all people of conscience facing conscienceless regimes.

"*Disturbing the Peace* leaves no room for controversy about [Havel's] place in the moral pantheon of our century."

—*The New York Times Book Review*

Autobiography/Current Affairs/0-679-73402-3/$11.00

OPEN LETTERS
Selected Writings 1965-1990

This collection of essays, letters, interviews, and reportage spanning twenty-five years shows Havel's evolution from a modestly known playwright with the courage to criticize his country's dictator to his becoming a newly elected president of Czechoslovakia.

"An inspiring collection...a fitting tribute to a cultural and political hero, and a valuable resource for anyone seeking reassurance that the principles of democracy are still cherished in our time."

—*Kirkus Reviews*

Current Affairs/Contemporary Politics/0-679-73811-8/$12.00